fundamentals
of
interpersonal
communication

under the advisory editorship of J. Jeffery Auer

# fundamentals
# of
# interpersonal
# communication

Kim Giffin
the university of kansas

Bobby R. Patton
the university of kansas

Harper & Row, Publishers, New York, Evanston, and London

Fundamentals of Interpersonal Communication

Copyright © 1971 by Kim Giffin and Bobby R. Patton

Printed in the United States of America. All rights reserved. No part of this book may be used or reproduced in any manner whatsoever without written permission except in the case of brief quotations embodied in critical articles and reviews. For information address Harper & Row, Publishers, Inc., 49 East 33rd Street, New York, N.Y. 10016.

Library of Congress Catalog Card Number: 76-125319

# contents

# preface

People in the 1970s are very much concerned about being *human* people—individuals able to have enjoyable relationships with other persons. Our automated, complex society has created a growing state of impersonality, and the yearning for closer personal ties is one of the major themes of our times.

Social and behavioral scientists have long been interested in the bases of such human interaction. The significant findings of the researchers, however, generally have been confined to graduate seminars and seldom translated into data valuable to the layman.

Communication is the foundation for all of our interpersonal relationships—its relevancy and significance for our lives can hardly be overemphasized. The purposes of this book are twofold: to present valid information on interpersonal communication to the student who possesses no specialized background; and to provide insights as to improving our relationships with others. To a large extent the study of interpersonal communication emphasizes the way in which a person intentionally communicates an idea to other people by the use of verbal symbols. In this book, however, we are also concerned with the processes by which the receiver interprets the motives of the speaker, the way in which the relationship between the two colors the interpretation of the message, ways in which the parties may attempt to change the relationship, and those environmental or cultural conditions which influence the effectiveness of these efforts at communication.

We are not concerned with theory for theory's sake, but rather with the research-based foundations for behavioral modification. By emphasizing the interactive, ongoing, process nature of interpersonal communication, we hope to acquaint the reader with the choices available for determining appropriate behavior. To the extent that the data is valid and reliable, individual judgments are necessary for personal applications.

It is our belief that each of us as a human being has personal needs which can only be satisfied by interaction with others. It is rather obvious but frequently overlooked that the degree to which a person does or does not interact with other people is usually taken as an index of his social maturation and/or mental health. A person who is physically capable of communicating with others, but utterly refuses to do so, is ordinarily viewed as mentally ill.

It is also our belief that the most important need for interpersonal communication is the achievement of personal growth and development—more specifically, the attainment of a desired self-image. A second need of perhaps equal importance is being able to negotiate with other people as we try to attain this personal growth and self-image.

We also believe that achievement of these goals is facilitated by obtaining new insights into one's present state of relationships with others. This involves understanding of (1) the nature of relationships that are potentially possible, and (2) reasons why such potentialities frequently have not been achieved.

In this book we have tried to present opportunities for the reader to understand better his basic needs for interpersonal communication, and for him to visualize the ways in which communication can be used to achieve more desirable relationships with others. It is our experience that when a person compares his own situation with a more desirable condition, he will then attempt to realize improvement through personal change.

Much of the material in this book is designed to give the reader information which can lead to new insights about himself and his current relationships with other people. However, such cognitive realization and insight is not enough—he must be encouraged to attempt behavioral change while his friends and associates provide a supportive climate. His efforts need to be directed specifically toward certain identifiable changes in his interpersonal behavior.

The Suggested Applications and Learning Experiences given at the end of each chapter are viewed as an integral part of this book and of great importance in helping the individual reader put into effect his new insights. *These learning experiences should be taken seriously by the reader as the principal way in which any new information can be made personally applicable to him.* He should recognize that although insight can enhance motivation to change behavior, only *attempts* to change that behavior along with *evaluation* of such attempts can make such knowledge personally useful. For this reason we strongly request our readers to participate in our suggested applications and learning experiences.

We are greatly indebted to the researchers who have provided the foundations for interpersonal communication principles presented in this book. We are also deeply grateful to our colleagues and associates who have encouraged our project.

# EFFORT AT SPEECH BETWEEN TWO PEOPLE

Muriel Rukeyser


*Speak to me.   Take my hand.   What are you now?*
*I will tell you all.   I will conceal nothing.*
*When I was three, a little child read a story about a rabbit*
*who died, in the story, and I crawled under a chair:*

*a pink rabbit:   it was my birthday, and a candle*
*burnt a sore spot on my finger, and I was told to be happy.*

*Oh, grow to know me.   I am not happy.   I will be open:*
*Now I am thinking of white sails against a sky like music,*
*like glad horns blowing, and birds tilting, and an arm about me.*
*There was one I loved, who wanted to live, sailing.*

From *Theory of Flight.* Reprinted by permission of International Famous Agency, Inc. Copyright 1935 by Yale University. Copyright © 1960 by Muriel Rukeyser.

Speak to me.   Take my hand.   What are you now?
When I was nine, I was fruitily sentimental,
fluid: and my widowed aunt played Chopin,
and I bent my head on the painted woodwork, and wept.
I want now to be close to you.   I would
link the minutes of my days close, somehow, to your days.

I am not happy.   I will be open.
I have liked lamps in evening corners, and quiet poems.
There has been fear in my life.   Sometimes I speculate
On what a tragedy his life was, really.

Take my hand.   Fist my mind in your hand.   What are you now?
When I was fourteen, I had dreams of suicide,
and I stood at a steep window, at sunset, hoping toward death:
if the light had not melted clouds and plains to beauty,
if light had not transformed that day, I would have leapt.
I am unhappy.   I am lonely.   Speak to me.

I will be open.   I think he never loved me:
he loved the bright beaches, the little lips of foam
that ride small waves, he loved the veer of gulls:
he said with a gay mouth: I love you.   Grow to know me.

What are you now?   If we could touch one another,
if these our separate entities could come to grips,
clenched like a Chinese puzzle . . . yesterday
I stood in a crowded street that was live with people,
and no one spoke a word, and the morning shone.
Everyone silent, moving. . . . Take my hand.   Speak to me.

fundamentals
of
interpersonal
communication

# principles of interpersonal communication | 1

Our lives are based upon our relationships with other people, and these relationships depend upon communication. So thoroughly do we take this interpersonal communication for granted that it scarcely ever occurs to us to examine the nature of it. We usually learn to communicate without much conscious effort, and by the time we are mature enough to understand the symbolism of actions and sounds that provide the basis for our interaction with others, it has become so much like reflex behavior, such as breathing, coughing, or chewing, that it hardly occurs to us there is anything to be understood. Our world of interactions with others, to which we have become so unreflectively accustomed, is indeed not something to be taken for granted.

The oft parodied phrase "failure to communicate" has become a byword in our complex society, whether used in the context of our diplomatic relations with other nations, in the midst of racial strife, in broken negotiations between labor and management, in arguments in the divorce courts, by student groups seeking more campus power from the administration, or in our day-to-day dealings with the people around us. In fact, interpersonal communication is the most important process in our lives. As human beings, we no longer live simply as a result of the products of our own hands, but through our dealings with others.

## A DEFINITION OF "INTERPERSONAL COMMUNICATION"

If each reader were asked to stop here and offer his definition of "communication," we might discover an assortment of potentially valid interpretations of this commonly used word. Even authorities vary in their conceptions of the term. Technical definitions abound.

Political scientist Harold Lasswell, interested in mass-media analysis, proposed five questions to indicate what he felt to be the important variables in communication:

Who?
*Says* What?
*In* Which Channel?
*To* Whom?
*With* What Effect?[1]

These five variables have become accepted criteria for describing and evaluating human communication.

At approximately the same time that Lasswell was preparing his model for overviewing human communication, two mathematicians, Shannon and Weaver, were developing a schematic model useful in analyzing such nonhuman communication as that involving computers, electrical circuiting, and energy transmission. Their model, shown in Figure 1, exposes some vital components of communication.

This model was flexible enough to suggest modifications to students of human communication through simple terminology adaptation. The "Information Source" became the "Sender of the Message" or the "Speaker." Sometimes a stimulus was introduced to show that the speaker was motivated to send the message. The "Transmitter" was taken to represent the "Encoder of the Message" whereas the "Receiver" became the "Decoder." The "Signal" be-

---

[1]H. D. Lasswell, "The Structure and Function of Communications in Society," in L. Bryson, ed., *The Communication of Ideas*, New York, Harper & Row, 1948, p. 37.

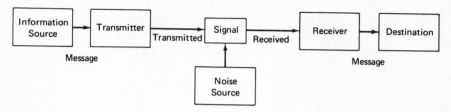

FIGURE 1 SHANNON-WEAVER MODEL OF COMMUNICATION. From C. E. Shannon and W. Weaver, *Theory of Communication,* Urbana, Ill., University of Illinois Press, 1949, p. 98. By permission.

came "Meaning." "Noise" was interpreted in a variety of ways ranging from simple situational disturbances to the more systematic problems of meaning embodied in semantics. The "Destination" was made in turn the "Receiver of the Message," with notations of potential response sometimes added.

One omission in the model was noted which actually altered the total conceptualization. The Shannon–Weaver model is linear in nature; that is, it visualizes communication as being initiated at one point and terminated at another along the given line. Largely as a result of the work of Norbert Wiener in cybernetics, the importance of "feedback" was noted.[2] He pointed out that communication is actually circular rather than linear, since output and input of circuits are linked as a means of mutually controlling the performance. In other words, positive feedback reinforces successful actions while negative feedback points out errors or inefficiencies. This feedback is important in human communication as means for a sender to check the success of his intended message by observing the reactions of the receiver.

But does identification of components actually tell us *what* "communication" is? A key to understanding the complexity of human communication lies in our conception of communication as *process.* As David K. Berlo, a leading communication theorist, has stated:

> *A communication theorist rejects the possibility that nature consists of events or ingredients that are separable from all other events. He argues that you cannot talk about the beginning or the end of communication or say that a particular*

[2]N. Wiener, *The Human Use of Human Beings,* Boston, Houghton Mifflin, 1954.

*idea came from one specific source, that communication occurs in only one way, and so on. . . . With the concept of process established in our minds, we can profit from an analysis of the ingredients of communication, the elements that seem necessary (if not sufficient) for communication to occur.*[3]

Later, in discussing the "Sender-Message-Receiver" model, he adds:

*The behaviors of the source do not occur independently of the behaviors of the receiver or vice versa. In any communication situation, the source and the receiver are interdependent.*[4]

This generally accepted view of communication permits us an opportunity to overview the total process rather than merely a collection of variables.

Such a process orientation was included in the model developed by Raymond Ross (Figure 2), which is an attempt to include human attributes in a view of the communication process.[5] The Ross model identifies not only variables found on the part of sender, receiver, and message, but also such situational variables as climate, situation, and culture.

Probably no one model will ever be able to identify all the potential variables in human communication, for even if it were possible to apply labels to all conceivable elements, the size and complexity of the model would make it useless. For our purposes, however, we should recognize that communication is a *dynamic process*, constantly changing, never static. All variables are constantly interacting with one another, modifying and adapting to all situational modifications. Although we may focus attention upon one or another of the variables, we must remember the fluid nature of the total process. As we examine interpersonal communication from a number of perspectives, different models will be utilized to help clarify views of particular variables.

For our purposes, then, communication may be viewed as a

[3]D. K. Berlo, *The Process of Communication*, New York, Holt, Rinehart and Winston, 1960, pp. 24–28.
[4]*Ibid.*, p. 106.
[5]R. S. Ross, *Speech Communication Fundamentals and Practice*, Englewood Cliffs, N.J., Prentice-Hall, 1965, p. 8.

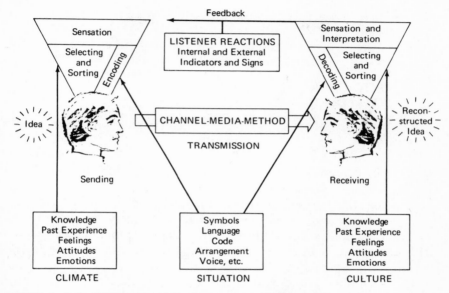

FIGURE 2    THE RAYMOND ROSS MODEL OF HUMAN COMMUNICATION. From Raymond S. Ross, *Speech Communication Fundamentals and Practice*, Englewood Cliffs, N.J., Prentice-Hall, 1965, p. 8. By permission.

process involving the sending and receiving of messages. To add the preface term "interpersonal" focuses attention on a special type of human communication. For contrast, we are not primarily concerned with "intrapersonal communication," that which transpires within an individual. Likewise we are not primarily concerned with speaker-audience communication, a situation in which one person is designated as a speaker and preplans his message, while his listeners are designated as an audience whose task it is to listen. Common examples of this category of human communication are classroom lectures and Sunday sermons. By "interpersonal communication" we are concerned with the face-to-face confrontations between people who are consistently aware of one another. Each person assumes roles as both sender and receiver of messages, which involves constant adaptation and spontaneous adjustment to the other person.

While "interpersonal communication" shares many common characteristics with other forms of human communication, it is unique in a number of ways. We should look at these basic characteristics in some detail.[6]

## BASIC CHARACTERISTICS OF INTERPERSONAL COMMUNICATION

1. *Interpersonal communication is inevitable when two people are together.*

This principle could hardly be more basic. In an interpersonal encounter, it is impossible not to communicate. Just as human behavior has no opposite, there can be no such thing as noncommunicating. If in an interpersonal situation the other person is aware of us at all, any and all behavior can have message value. Both words and silence, both activity and inactivity have communication potential. And as our behavior influences others, they are likewise forced to communicate by their response to us.

It should be understood that the mere absence of talking or refusing to take notice of another person is no exception to this rule. The man at the crowded lunch counter who looks straight ahead or the person on a train who sits with his eyes closed are both communicating. Probably the message they are sending is that they do not want to talk to anybody; other people usually understand the message and respond appropriately by leaving them alone.

Neither can we say that communication only takes place when it is conscious or intentional, much less when it is successful. Whether or not mutual understanding results, and whether or not we anticipate a desired response from another person, we are communicating. This impossibility of not communicating is a principle of more than theoretical interest; it is the basis for potential misunderstanding. The withdrawn teen-ager, who sometimes appears to be a problem to his parents or his teachers may be no problem at all to himself. He may be thinking that his communication behavior is not one which implies a problem to anyone else. His own thoughts may be, "I would like privacy"; he simply would prefer to be left alone. This message, how-

---

[6]These characteristics are postulated as axioms in P. Watzlawick, J. H. Beavin, and D. D. Johnson, *Pragmatics of Human Communication*, New York, Norton, 1967, pp. 48–71.

ever may be interpreted by a parent or teacher as, "I want to be antisocial."

2. *Interpersonal communication includes both content and information about the content.*

Communication is not merely by words alone. The choice of words, the tone of voice, and bodily action all communicate a variety of messages. Two persons may say "Good morning" to each other and convey a number of messages. One "Good morning" may indicate supplication, awareness of subordinate status, anxiety as to how the greeting will be received, etc. The other may convey condescension, awareness of power position, rejection, hostility, etc.

This information about the content of the message being transmitted is called metacommunication; it consists of nonverbal qualifiers or interpretational signals about the verbal message—what is really meant, or how it is to be understood. Clinical psychologist Jurgen Reusch identifies the two communicational operations as the "report" and the "command" aspects respectively of any communicative act. He exemplifies these two aspects by means of a physiological analogy: Let A, B, and C be a linear chain of neurons. Then the firing of neuron B is both a report that neuron A has fired and a command for neuron C to fire. The "report" aspect of a message conveys information and is therefore inseparable in human communication from the content of the message. This content may be true, false, valid, invalid, or indecisive. The "command" aspect of the message refers to information as to what sort of message it is taken to be.[7]

In one sense, the "command" aspect indicates the relationship between the communicants. Such relationship messages may indicate how I see myself, how I see you, how I see you seeing me, etc., to theoretical infinity. Thus, the verbal message, "Will you please close the door?" is quite different from "Just leave the door open and everybody will be drifting in." The second message remains ambiguous until metacommunication is supplied and relationship is understood.

Interpersonal relationships are seldom defined deliberately with full awareness and in plain language. In fact, it seems that the more spontaneous and automatic the relationship is, the more pleas-

[7]J. Reusch and G. Bateson, *Communication: The Social Matrix of Psychiatry,* New York, Norton, 1951, pp. 179–181.

ant and healthier. Conversely, unhealthy relations may be characterized by a constant struggle between the participants to define the nature of their relationship with the "report" aspect of the message becoming less and less important. Attention is focused not on what was said but rather on "Why did you say it?"

When the "report" and "command" aspects of the message do not fit, the receiver must somehow translate the data into a single message. A husband—for example one who has been working in the yard—comes into the house and says to his wife in an irritable tone of voice, "Damn it, the shovel handle broke!" The wife must then, with great agility and skill go through the following process:

a. He is reporting on the condition of the shovel.

b. I know that he is irritated. His "Damn it," and the tone of his voice make this clear.

c. Is he blaming me for the condition of the shovel? If he is criticizing me, what does he think I should do—apologize, help him, or what?

d. Maybe he is criticizing himself and is frustrated by the broken handle. If so, what is he asking me to do—sympathize, just listen, or what?

e. Since I know from living with him that he has little patience with malfunctions, he is probably just irritated at the situation and is asking me primarily to sympathize with him.

f. Now how can I communicate that I am genuinely sympathetic—listen quietly, offer to help, bring him coffee, offer suggestions? How can I best communicate my conscious concern and interest?

Had the husband merely said "I'm having a hard time in the yard. Bring me a cup of coffee," the wife would have had little difficulty assessing the message. She is still in the position of deciding whether or not to agree to the husband's request, but at least she is not in doubt as to what he wants of her.[8]

It is not uncommon, at least in the movies, to see two soldiers talking with one another. One of them makes a statement and then says, "That is an order." In such a case, the superior takes special pains to insure that the information content and the information

[8]This exchange and analysis is suggested by V. Satir, *Conjoint Family Therapy*, Palo Alto, Calif., Science and Behavior, 1967, p. 79.

about the content are both clearly understood. In other cases we may see two individuals conversing and when a crisis appears imminent, one of them says, "Of course, you realize I'm only joking," or his behavior conveys this same message.

The metacommunication must be perfectly clear for successful transference of messages between individuals. If the content of the message seems to indicate one kind of interpersonal relationship and the metacommunication seems to indicate another kind, communication barriers, misunderstanding, and other problems may arise. No doubt we all have had dealings with people when we could not tell for certain whether they were joking or serious. A note reading "Please go to see the Dean as soon as possible," could be confusing in its implications. If this message were spoken, we would have less difficulty determining how we should respond. The ability to convey and interpret metacommunication cues is vital to successful interpersonal communication.

3. *The "punctuation" of a series of interpersonal interactions affects the meanings conveyed.*

Too often the process of interpersonal communication is viewed as an uninterrupted sequence of exchanges. The participants, however, identify portions of these exchanges in different ways. Just as in written material we use punctuation to divide a message into coherent discourse and properly subordinate ideas, so in oral interpersonal communication we punctuate a series of interchanges with another person and interpret our relationship to him. If the relationship is interpreted in the same way by both people, probably no difficulty will arise. Frequently, however, the individuals will identify interchanges as little sequences, so that it appears to one or the other that a given individual has initiative, dominance, dependency, and so forth. For example, the rat who said, "I have my experimenter well trained; each time I press the lever he gives me food," was declining to accept the sequence of events which the experimenter was identifying. While most rats, however, are too nice to refuse to identify sequence of interaction in the same way that a human being does, such is not the case with people. The identification of a series of interactions organizes one's perception of behavioral events and is extremely vital to ongoing interpersonal communication.

Culturally we share many conventions of identification of such series. Such identification is frequently in tune with the role of other people. For example, we may have a congruent view of our relationship with our employer, identifying him as leader and ourselves as followers; when he speaks, we respond; and as we respond, we expect him to speak again and us to respond again. If, however, boss and employee are in disagreement about who is responding to whom, difficulty is likely to arise.

Consider a couple having marital difficulties. Suppose that the husband generally shows passive withdrawal and then reentry into the communication situation. In explaining the couple's disagreements and frustrations, he will indicate that withdrawal is his only defense against her nagging. He will indicate that she nags, he withdraws; he goes back into the situation, she nags, and he withdraws. The wife's interpretation of the interaction sequences will very likely be, however, that he withdraws, and she has to nag to get him back into talking with her. Their two interpretations may be identified as:

a. "I withdraw because you nag."
b. "I nag because you withdraw."

Seldom, however, do people recognize such a problem or talk about these things.

Thus, the nature of a relationship is contingent upon the punctuation of the communication sequences between the communicators.

4. *Nonverbal communication ultimately defines an interpersonal relationship.*

This term "nonverbal communication" includes postures, gestures, rhythm and cadence of the words themselves, and all other nonverbal manifestations of which a person is capable. It also includes all of the communication clues which are present in any context in which an interaction occurs. These cues are considered to be of greater general validity than the more abstract linguistic codes of verbal communication. The truth of this observation can be verified by our tendency to "believe" nonverbal communication cues should they be incongruous with the linguistic message. For example, even the words "I hate you" can be made to sound and appear seductive.

Nonverbal communication can sometimes carry a direct message; at other times, it may function as metacommunication, that is, information indicating how to interpret a verbal message. In either

case, nonverbal communication generally is taken to be highly indicative of the true relationship between two people.

A husband says, "There's nothing the matter" to his wife in a strained, tense voice as if holding back tears or an explosion of anger. Is the wife likely to respond to his words or to the message sent nonverbally? A father says that his son should not defy him; yet he also complains that his son doesn't stand up to him like a man. A well-known observation of psychotherapists is that when a relationship goes wrong, turns sour, or becomes sick, much communication is conveyed concerning the nature of the relationship. The individuals involved spend endless amounts of time quibbling and quarreling over what they think of each other and how their behavior can be construed to mean they still care for each other. While the linguistic code may reinforce this notion, the behavioral or nonverbal level indicates quite clearly that the relationship is in trouble.

Behavior in an interpersonal situation speaks louder than words and is more readily accepted. Such nonverbal communication similarly establishes the basis for interaction in the animal world and for animal interaction with humans. In research with bottle-nose porpoises, investigators have noted the unique way in which the porpoise attempts to establish a relationship with humans. The animal attempts to take a person's hand in its mouth and gently squeeze the hand in its powerful jaws of razor-sharp teeth. If the human will submit to this demonstration, the porpoise seems to accept the act as a message of complete trust. His next move is to reciprocate by placing the forward, bent portion of his body, roughly equivalent to the human throat—his most vulnerable area—upon the man's hand, foot, or leg, thereby signaling his trust in the friendly intentions of the person. Similarly, a cat routinely establishes a demonstration of trust through the ritual of throwing himself on his back, exposing his jugular vein to younger cats or cats from outside his own territory. The taking of the jugular vein in the jaw of the other cat establishes an "I shall not attack you" message which serves to define the relationship.[9]

While language can be used to communicate almost anything, nonverbal behavior is rather limited in range. It is usually used to

[9]Watzlawick et al., op. cit., p. 104.

communicate feelings, likings, and preferences and to reinforce or contradict the feelings that are communicated verbally. It may add a new dimension to the verbal message as when a salesman describes his product to a client and simultaneously conveys, nonverbally, the impression that he likes the client.

Nonverbal messages can, like linguistic ones, be misinterpreted. A husband, for example, may find himself suspected of an unconfessed guilt if he spontaneously presents his wife with a bouquet of flowers. Sometimes we are confused in trying to interpret the meaning of growing pale, trembling, sweating, or stammering by a person who is being questioned. It can be interpreted as unmistakable proof of guilt or it may merely be the behavior of an innocent person going through the experience of being suspected and realizing his fear may be interpreted as guilt. We add to the potential confusion by our propensity to "play games" with our outward manifestations of feelings. We have become good "poker faces" and are to a great extent, able to conceal our genuine feelings.

The way in which we interpret another person's reactions to us in the form of nonverbal messages determines our relationship with him. His acceptance of us in turn causes us to accept him. The cues are constantly being reinterpreted and reanalyzed at our subconscious level as the basis for future interaction.

5. *Interpersonal communication is based upon a constant, progressive pattern of reactions.*

An interpersonal communication interaction tends to follow a fluid, predictable pattern. The typical pattern is either complementary or symmetrical. In the first relationship, one person's behavior complements that of the other person, forming what might be viewed as a behavioral "gestalt." If one is assertive, the other will likely be submissive; that is, unless other factors are present to restrain excesses, A will become more and more assertive, and B will become more and more permissive.

In the second pattern, the persons in the relationship tend to mirror each other's behavior to balance one another. If, for example, one seems to be bent upon becoming the stronger of the two, and the other person replies to this with attempts to maintain his own strength, a competitive situation will develop. Such a symmetrical relationship will tend to produce more and more attempts on the part of both members to strengthen their positions of leadership unless restraining factors are also present./

The terms complementary and symmetrical should not be thought of in good-bad or right-wrong terms. The two are merely descriptive of the communicative interaction and, depending upon the personalities of the communicants, may establish the basis for the sustaining of a relationship.

In some ongoing interactions, the "one-up" and "one-down" positions may quickly and easily be reversed so that a complementary total relationship is established. An individual says, "Oh, did you hear about . . . ?" and the other person listens attentively. Both parties may profit from the interchange. The roles reverse and the listener says, "Yes, but did you know . . . ?" as the first person becomes the listener. This kind of interaction, where the relationship is fluid and changing, can be a profitable, normal relationship for both people. While competition may develop for the role of message sender, the other person willingly becomes a receiver for a complementary communication pattern.

In any symmetrical relationship, there is the ever-present danger of extreme competitiveness. This tendency accounts for the typical escalating quality of symmetrical interactions into runaways once stability is lost: quarrels, fights, and broken relationships result. When sweethearts lose the sense of belonging to a total relationship and compete for individual gratification alone, the relationship will be short-lived.

Similarly a complementary relationship can also degenerate. A problem may result when A demands that B confirm a definition of himself that is at variance with the way B sees himself. B is placed in a dilemma; he must either change his own self-definition or modify A's view. Husbands and wives may encounter such a problem in the transition from courtship to marriage. A woman who has been content to be a submissive follower during courtship may not wish to retain such a complementary role to a dominant husband forever. Problems likewise occur in the business world over the role of leader or subordinates, even among "equals"!

At any given time, the pattern of interpersonal reactions may be designated as complementary or symmetrical, but in the long chain of encounters these patterns may revolve and adjust.

## SUMMARY AND PROJECTIONS

These five characteristics should provide us with an overview of the facets of interpersonal communication that we will discuss in the remainder of this book.

In Chapter 2 we shall examine the "whys" of interpersonal communication. Since communication is inevitable when two people are together, why does one person endeavor to elicit a response from the other? We have labeled this inevitability as the "communication imperative."

The basis for the interpersonal exchange is the way in which the two people view each other—their interpersonal perception. This will be the focus of Chapter 3.

Over a period of time, we develop a general overall orientation toward people that determines the way we attempt to communicate. The "constant, progressive pattern of reactions," based upon the personalities of the communicators, will be the topic for Chapter 4.

Based upon our desire to communicate, our perception of the other person, and our orientation toward him, we encode linguistic messages to him and decode his responses to us. The way in which we employ language, the quality of our inferences, and the way in which we structure messages will be discussed in Chapter 5.

All interpersonal communication takes place in physical-social situations which affect the way in which a message is sent and received. We are influenced by such factors as role, time pressures, stress, presence of others, and channels of communication available to us. These variables will be considered in Chapter 6.

Effective interpersonal communication is possible only after certain barriers have been overcome. "Gaps" between people from different backgrounds, defensive communication, and feelings of alienation greatly impair our communication potential. The ways in which interpersonal trust and a helping relationship can be established will be the focus of Chapter 7.

Finally, in Chapter 8, we shall attempt to determine certain guidelines which will improve our interpersonal communicative skills.

Since each reader is a unique, individualized communicator with abilities and problems different from every other person, personal adaptations and applications must be made as one reads. The contents of the chapters are meaningful only to the extent that one can see personal, practical implications that can serve as the potential for improved communication capabilities.

## Suggested Applications and Learning Experiences

1. In groups of two or three, design a situation involving hidden conflict. *Who* you are, *where* you are, and *what* you are doing must be agreed upon. Each of you is to decide on a point of conflict that you will never verbalize as you role-play with the other participants.

**Example:**    *Where—kitchen; Who—husband and wife;*
*What—breakfast.*
*Hidden conflict: Husband—I'm not going to work today.*
          *Wife—I want him to leave. I'm expecting*
                   *a visitor.*

Diagnose your capabilities to interpret the basis for conflict and discuss situations involving such problems.

2. Meet in groups of five or six people. Using the Ross model as a basis for discussion, attempt to formulate a model that you think represents your interpersonal communication. What components do you feel are indispensable and which vary from situation to situation?

3. Individually or in groups view a drama on television with the sound turned off. Attempt to formulate the relationships between the characters by the nonverbal cues. Contrast this experience to radio dramas where we receive only the verbal message. Under what circumstances is one alternative more interesting than the other? Consider the degree of communication potential in silent films.

4. Analyze an interaction in which you have been involved recently from a viewpoint of "punctuation." What nonverbal cues communicate that we are finished with a message and want someone else to talk? Similarly, how do we supply feedback to the speaker that "now I want to talk."

5. Eye behavior is one of the most potent elements in our non-

verbal behavior. Our normal eye contacts last only about a second, and we are quite careful about how and when we look someone directly in the eye. Intercultural communication researchers have noted the differences between cultures and subcultures on the amount and types of interpersonal eye contacts. What have you noted of these differences? As an exercise, work in pairs and sit facing each other for a period of about three minutes, saying nothing and looking each other intently in the eyes. Discuss your reactions. What were you able to communicate?

### Suggested Readings

*Barnlund, Dean C., "Toward a Meaning-Centered Philosophy of Communication," *Journal of Communication, 11* (1962), 197–204.

Berlo, David K., "A Model of the Communicative Process," *The Process of Communication,* New York, Holt, Rinehart and Winston, 1960, pp. 23–39.

*Ruesch, Jurgen, "Communication and Human Relations: An Interdisciplinary Approach," in Jurgen Ruesch and Gregory Bateson, *Communication: The Social Matrix of Psychiatry,* New York, Norton, 1968, pp. 21–38.

*Satir, Virginia, "Communication: A Verbal and Nonverbal Process of Making Requests of the Receiver," *Conjoint Family Therapy,* rev. ed., Palo Alto, Calif., Science and Behavior Books, 1967, pp. 75–90.

Watzlawick, Paul, Janet H. Beavin, and Don D. Jackson, "Some Tentative Axioms of Communication," *Pragmatics of Human Communication,* New York, Norton, 1967, pp. 48–71.

*Items thus identified are reprinted in Kim Giffin and Bobby R. Patton, *Basic Readings in Interpersonal Communication,* New York, Harper & Row, 1971.

# the
# interpersonal 2
# imperative

In Chapter 1, we discussed communication from a number of perspectives and compared various definitions of the process. In this chapter we shall focus attention upon the sender of the message, the initiator of the communication. As a person attempts to elicit a response from another, he is responding to some motive that causes him to want to communicate. Such behavior is so automatic that we rarely stop to analyze our motives. It should be helpful to our understanding of interpersonal communication to identify and categorize the basic motives commonly underlying it.

Our approach will be what is called by scholars a "phenomenological" one; that is, we will look at the needs of the individual as *he perceives them*, rather than as perceived by someone else *for him*. The way in which an individual perceives his needs—real or otherwise—provides the basis of motivation for him to do something about them.

## PERSONAL DEVELOPMENT THROUGH COMMUNICATION

While it is obvious that we employ communication to develop ourselves, the ways in which we attempt such personal development should be explored in some detail.

## The Search for Socially Approved Ways of Behaving

One of the first areas of personal development is to discover ways of behaving which win the approval of other people. At an early age this response is sought ordinarily from one's parents; later it involves friends, teachers, employers, and membership groups. Our behavior is determined by what social scientists call *the discovery of socially approved "norms" of behavior.*

As we grow and develop, we need to know how to get along in the world; we need to discover what we can do well and the ways in which we are limited or less competent. We need to determine what other people are like, how they view us, and how they will respond to our efforts to find our way through life. In effect, we are motivated to discover all we can about ourselves and the people around us through interpersonal communication with them.

Our motivations are threefold. One of our purposes is *to determine the nature of our surroundings*—to sort out things that satisfy basic needs such as hunger or thirst, things which are pleasing to hear or touch, and of course, things which are enjoyable to eat or taste. A second objective is *to determine ways in which we can achieve the cooperation of other people.* We find this necessary both to satisfy basic needs and while doing so to enjoy our relationships with other people. The third objective is *to check our findings by comparing them with the perceptions of others.* We do this by noting the various kinds of feedback we receive regarding our behavior.

In 1954, Leon Festinger wrote an essay that provided the basis for a large number of research studies.[1] In this essay Festinger described his view of the way a person confirms his impressions of his environment. Festinger identified a continuum on which he placed "physical reality" at one end and "social reality" on the other.

Physical reality was said to involve such things as objects or surfaces, the perception of which an individual can validate with his physiological senses. Social reality was said to involve perceptions of such things as appropriate social behavior, judgments of a moral or ethical nature, those elements of reality we usually associate with attitudes, opinions, or beliefs. An opinion, attitude, or belief was said to be perceived by the individual as valid to the extent it was

[1]L. Festinger, "A Theory of Social Comparison Processes," *Human Relations,* 7 (1954), 117–140.

anchored in (or reflected by) an approved reference group. For example, the validation of one's perception of himself as an "adequate communicator" would require, at least in part, positive feedback from other people.

There are many areas in which our perceptions need to be checked by comparison with those of others through interpersonal communication. We do this each time we change to a new environment; for example, when we enter a different school, take a new job, or become a new member of a group, we ask others about norm-expectancies. In groups and organizations certain people may be identified as "norm-givers"—those who take responsibility for giving us orientations; frequently such people tell us how we are doing as we adjust to the new environment.

In thus comparing ourselves with others we tend to seek information about persons who are somewhat similar to us. We seek information about people similar to us or even a little above us when the characteristic in question is highly valued; for example, the ability to do well on an examination.[2] We tend to seek information about those a little less confident than ourselves when evaluating our fear or our behavior in a situation which we see as threatening.[3] We tend to seek information about others who are closely similar to us when we have some reason to be unsure of our ability.[4] And in the absence of information about other persons, we tend to make inaccurate and unstable self-evaluations.[5]

This process of discovering socially approved norms of behavior never ends. We continuously want to be sure we are doing the right thing, and doing it well—that is, doing it in a way which will win the continued cooperation of others in satisfying such needs.

As we search for socially approved norms, we find it necessary to resolve our confusion when we receive conflicting feedback from

[2]L. Wheeler, "Motivation as a Determinant of Upward Comparison," Journal of Experimental Social Psychology Supplement, 1 (1966), 27–32.

[3]J. M. Darley and E. Aronson, "Self-evaluation vs. Direct Anxiety Reduction as Determinants of the Fear-Affiliation Relationship," Journal of Experimental Social Psychology Supplement, 1 (1966), 66–70.

[4]K. Hakmiller, "Need for Self-Evaluation, Perceived Similarity and Comparison Choice," Journal of Experimental Social Psychology Supplement, 1 (1966), 49–54.

[5]R. Radloff, "Social Comparison and Ability Evaluation," Journal of Experimental Social Psychology Supplement, 1 (1966), 6–26.

others regarding our behavior. Studies of this problem have generally been reported under the rubric of *resolving cognitive dissonance.* This general concept applies to all of our perceptions, those related to physical reality as well as the ones directly relating to our self-evaluations.

Three theories of cognitive consistency have received wide attention: The "balance theory" of Heider,[6] the "congruity theory" of Osgood,[7] and the "cognitive dissonance theory" of Festinger.[8] The three consistency theories are somewhat different, but have one thing in common: they assert that the normal condition of a person's attitudes is that of internal consistency between elements perceived as related, and that attitude change is the reduction of dissonance generated by new communications about, or new perceptions of, an attitude object.

Perhaps an example taken from a research report can illustrate the use of interpersonal communication to resolve problems of conflicting feedback about our behavior. In a manufacturing plant which was part of a nationally known industrial complex, a small item was being produced under a federal government contract. This contract required that all workmen at the plant wear conspicuous identification badges at all times. Compliance with this ruling had been lacking; some of the men said they thought the brightly colored official badges "looked silly." Interviews showed that company officials were telling the men that the badges must be worn. An inventory of attitudes toward wearing the badges showed that most of the men held negative attitudes. The experimenters arranged for discussion of the topic by randomly selected groups of workmen; workmen not selected were treated as a "control" group—the basis for comparison. The experimental groups were asked to "meet and discuss the topic of identification badges"—no additional instructions nor leadership were provided. The kind of communication employed was not controlled by the experimenter (nor by management); details of the discussion sessions reflected the decisions of the individuals involved. It

[6]F. Heider, "Attitudes and Cognitive Organization," *Journal of Psychology,* 21 (1946), 107–112; see also, F. Heider, *The Psychology of Interpersonal Relations,* New York, Wiley, 1958.
[7]C. E. Osgood, G. J. Suci, and P. H. Tannenbaum, *The Measurement of Meaning,* Urbana, Ill., Univ. of Illinois Press, 1957.
[8]L. Festinger, *A Theory of Cognitive Dissonance,* New York, Harper & Row, 1957.

was inferred that there was sufficient cognitive dissonance to motivate group interaction; the group members did talk about the badges and related considerations—federal contracts, rulings, need for individual identification, etc.

The results showed that the persons in the experimental groups who had discussed the badges for about an hour showed significant changes in attitudes (favorable) as measured by post-testing; their post-test attitudes were significantly different from the post-test attitudes of the control group; and the members of the experimental group were later reported by the company officials to have significantly increased the amount of wearing the badges. Post-experiment interviews indicated that the men found that although the individual's evaluation of *himself* when he wore the badge was that he "looked silly," most persons' evaluation of the looks of *another* person's wearing the badge was that he did *not* "look silly"—given the contract conditions existing at that plant. In this experiment it appeared that cognitive dissonance regarding badges was reduced by interpersonal communication.[9]

### The Search for Self-Identity

We all have ideas about who and what we are; taken together these beliefs are our self-image or identity. Some persons, particularly adolescents, seem to be desperately struggling to define themselves. Other persons seem to know what they are, but are most concerned about what they might hope to become.

With respect to this identity-formation, it is useful to note the contribution of G. H. Mead; perhaps more than any other theorist he viewed the development of self-identity as the product of social interaction. Mead emphasized the importance of face-to-face interpersonal communication—how we respond to others and they in turn respond to us. In this way we learn about ourselves; each interchange gives us cues about how others see us and this shapes our view of ourselves. From the time we are small children this process goes on; virtually all communication to us gives us indications of our importance, capabilities, and potential, as well as our inadequacies.[10]

---

[9]K. Giffin and L. Ehrlich, "The Attitudinal Effects of a Group Discussion on a Proposed Change in Company Policy," *Speech Monographs, 30* (1963), 337–379.

[10]G. H. Mead, *Mind, Self and Society,* Chicago, Univ. of Chicago Press, 1934, pp. 144–164.

The following description of the process of identity formation has been given by another very well-recognized theorist on self-identity, Erik Erikson:

> . . . identity formation . . . is a lifelong development largely unconscious to the individual and to his society. Its roots go back all the way to the first self-recognition: in the baby's earliest exchange of smiles there is something of a self-realization coupled with a mutual recognition.[11]

The process of identity-formation via interaction with others, suggested by Mead and Erikson, is largely a reflection of the perception of us by others. Cooley coined the phrase "the looking-glass self" and Sullivan spoke of "reflected self-appraisal." These are graphic labels for this process.

Of course, not all beliefs about ourselves are formed by social interaction. Direct sensory perception tells us when we are tired, hungry, or burn our finger. Also, Festinger's social-comparison process tells us when we are as tall as our parents, weigh more than "the average," or work arithmetic problems "faster than most" persons. Even so, *the choice of persons with whom we make such comparisons* is largely shaped by social interaction with persons in close relation to us.[12] There are some indications that as we pass from childhood into adulthood, more and more of our beliefs about ourselves are formed through feedback about ourselves from others and employed by us for comparing ourselves with norms, averages, and members of reference groups.[13]

As children we like to have our parents give us things, but most of all we want them to *communicate* with us. We do not know for certain what we are until others (significant to us) tell us. We even prefer mild punishment to total indifference; in later life we can tolerate hate better than we can accept total neglect.[14]

Even in the pain of being hated we can at least know that we really exist. Socrates, condemned to death, faced condemnation with

[11]E. Erikson, "The Problem of Ego Identity," *Psychological Issues, 1* (1959), 47.

[12]B. Latane, "Studies in Social Comparison—Introduction and Overview," *Journal of Experimental Social Psychology Supplement, 1* (1966), 1–5.

[13]Radloff, *op. cit.*, 6–26.

[14]H. Duncan, *Communication and Social Order*, New York, Oxford Univ. Press, 1962, pp. 271–273.

WHEN I WAS VERY YOUNG I WAS TOTALLY SELF-ORIENTED. I FELT THAT WHEN I ENTERED A CROWDED ROOM I WAS REALLY **THE ONLY** PERSON THERE.

AND THAT WHEN I LEFT THE ROOM ALL THE PEOPLE BEHIND ME **CEASED** TO EXIST.

THEN AS I GREW A LITTLE OLDER AND LEARNED DISAPPOINTMENT I DEVELOPED THE **NEW** FEELING THAT WHEN I ENTERED A CROWDED ROOM—

—I WAS THE ONLY PERSON WHO **WASN'T** THERE.

From *Hold Me!*, by Jules Feiffer. Copyright © 1960, 1961, 1962 by Jules Feiffer. Reprinted by permission of Random House, Inc.

IN ALL OF LIFE IT SEEMED TO ME THAT I WAS THE **LEAST** REAL.

BUT OF COURSE GROWTH IS A CONTINUING PROCESS. AS THE YEARS WENT BY I **MELLOWED.** I NO LONGER LOOKED AT LIFE IN ABSOLUTES.

NOWADAYS WHEN I ENTER A CROWDED ROOM—

I'M NOT SURE **ANY** OF US ARE THERE.

pride and honor; he believed that his death would affect important future acts of his countrymen. But if no one responds to our acts or thoughts, while yet we cannot live without thinking and acting, the incongruity between our needs and our world becomes unbearable. Under such cimcumstances children aggress against their parents and teen-agers test authority by violating rules. In extreme circumstances a person may behave in extreme ways in order to obtain a response —any response—to establish his *existence,* regardless of the degree of antagonism or hostility his behavior will produce.

An unprovoked attack upon another person can never be condoned; however, the terrible sense of loneliness, neglect, and the need for some kind of attention from others which instigates such an attack is pertinent to the study of interpersonal communication. Attempted destruction of oneself may be a call for "help"—attention from and consequential interaction with others; it may also be the despondent conclusion that this need will never be met, that rewarding human interaction for such a person is impossible.

The important point to be understood is that almost every time we initiate communication, even on a nonverbal level, we are making an implied request: "Please confirm my viewpoint." Sometimes this request is actually spoken; usually, however, it is implied on the unspoken, nonverbal level. Sometimes it concerns our understanding of factual data or information; frequently, it involves confirmation of an opinion. Always there is an implicit request for evaluation of us as a person. We can summarize the point thus: *every time we initiate communication or respond to it, we also make this request: "Please validate me—confirm my viewpoint and indicate my value as a person."* In this fashion we use interpersonal communication to form an impression of our self-identity.

The maintenance of a self-image, once it is formed, is a continuing process. Our self-image is confirmed anew whenever another person responds to us. Mutual recognition of such self-image provides confirmation and maintenance.

If there is consistent social confirmation, a strong and integrated self-identity will be developed and sustained. In such a case there is less need to seek confirmatory responses or to shield ourselves from possible disconfirmation. This condition provides greater freedom for the individual to be spontaneous, creative—to live; there is no great need to be concerned about every little criticism or evaluation of one's behavior. Such a person can dare to hear feedback about who and what he is, and can frequently test the validity of his beliefs about himself.

On the other hand, a person whose self-image is frequently disconfirmed will almost continually seek information about it; he will need to hear feedback, but will fear it; he will seek it, and at the same time try to avoid it. His self-image will suffer either way: if he hears negative evaluation no matter how slight, he will likely feel anxiety; if he avoids evaluation he will derogate himself for being a coward—he's "damned if he does and damned if he doesn't" seek self-image confirmation. Someone very wise once said, "To him who hath shall be given, and from him who hath not shall be taken away." This principle very much applies to the maintenance of one's self-image. To a very large extent theories of non-directive counseling developed by Carl Rogers are attempts to break this vicious circle of need, fear, and avoidance of possible image-building feedback.[15]

There is little question of the importance to the individual of the continuing need for interpersonal communication which confirms one's self-image. Once is never enough. Men have developed elaborate social rituals to reduce the probability of disconfirmation. Children are taught to become "tactful," responding to other people in a way that does not challenge the validity of the self-image they present in public. Erving Goffman has written two very insightful essays on this general topic, one of which is on how to "save face."[16] His other essay relative to maintenance of self-image is on "cooling out the mark," i.e., ways people employ to soften the blow of disconfirmation of a person's self-image. The term "mark" is a colloquialism for the confidence man's target or dupe, and the point of the analogy is the way in which the dupe is "conned" into accepting his role as the con man's mark. A brief excerpt dealing with courtship and marriage relations will indicate the nature of Goffman's thesis.

[15]C. Rogers, *On Becoming a Person,* Boston, Houghton Mifflin, 1961.
[16]E. Goffman, "On Face-Work: An Analysis of Ritual Elements in Social Interaction," *Psychiatry, 18* (1955), 213–231.

IN THE PAST I FAVORED DIALOGUE WITH THE ESTABLISHMENT, BELIEVING THAT IN TIME IT WOULD LEAD, THROUGH A PROCESS OF CONCESSIONS, TO A GRADUAL ACCEPTANCE OF RADICAL CHANGE. THESE VIEWS NOTWITHSTANDING, MY EARLY DIALOGUES WITH THE ESTABLISHMENT PROVED WHOLLY DISAPPOINTING, THE OTHER SIDE ARGUING THAT THE AIRING OF DIFFERENCES WAS PROGRESS ENOUGH, MY SIDE HOLDING OUT FOR MEANINGFUL CHANGE. FURTHER DIALOGUES LED ONLY TO FURTHER MISUNDERSTANDINGS WHICH BECAME THE

SUBJECT FOR NEW DIALOGUES DURING WHICH PREVIOUS POSITIONS WERE RESTATED AND PREVIOUS CONCESSIONS REAFFIRMED, AND ONCE MORE NOT CARRIED OUT. SINCE DIALOGUES ARE MEANT TO SERVE AS A SAFETY VALVE AGAINST VIOLENCE, I WONDERED WHY THE MORE WE TALKED THE MORE I FELT BRUTALIZED, EVENTUALLY HAVING NO CHOICE BUT TO TURN INARTICULATE BECAUSE I WAS UNWILLING TO ADMIT THAT THE ONLY WORD I COULD THINK OF SAYING WAS: "KILL."

FOR THEIR SAKE
I HOPE THEY DO
NOT SUCCEED IN
REESTABLISHING
CONTACT.

FINALLY I WAS FORCED
TO STOP TALKING
IN ORDER NOT TO
START KILLING. THE
ESTABLISHMENT
BLAMES THE COL-
LAPSE OF OUR DIA-
LOGUES ON A
BREAKDOWN IN COM-
MUNICATION.

LIKE
MAN
Y'KNOW

*The problem of cooling persons out in informal social intercourse is seen most clearly, perhaps, in courting situations and in what might be called decourting situations. A proposal of marriage in our society tends to be a way in which a man sums up his social attributes and suggests to a woman that hers are not so much better as to preclude a merger or partnership in these matters. Refusal on the part of the woman, or refusal on the part of the man to propose when he is clearly in a position to do so, is a serious reflection on the rejected suitor. . . . Refusing a proposal, or refusing to propose, is therefore a difficult operation. The mark must be carefully cooled out. . . . Just as it is harder to refuse a proposal than to refuse a date, so it is more difficult to reject a spouse than to reject a suitor. The process of decourting by which one person in a marriage maneuvers the other into accepting a divorce without fuss or undue rancor requires extreme finesse in the art of cooling the mark out. . . . For the mark, cooling represents a process of adjustment to an impossible situation— a situation arising from having defined himself in a way which the social facts come to contradict. The mark must therefore be supplied with a new set of apologies for himself, a new framework in which to see himself and judge himself. A process of redefining the self along defensible lines must be instigated and carried along; since the mark himself is frequently in too weakened a condition to do this, the cooler must initially do it for him.*[17]

## The Development of Self-Esteem

The self-image one desires must be achieved in his own eyes. Confirmation of this self-image by feedback from others gives a person the feeling that he is entitled to have this image of himself. Continuing confirmation helps him to maintain and to clarify the image. In this sense the desired self-image is improved—it is perceived as more real, its wearer feels that it fits more comfortably, and the shadows of self-doubt are dispersed.

A desired self-image is the basis of self-esteem. A person acts

[17]E. Goffman, "On Cooling the Mark Out," *Psychiatry*, 15 (1952), 457–458.

and in doing so intentionally or unintentionally exposes his view of himself. Another person responds to this behavior; very frequently this response conveys approval or disapproval, acceptance or rejection. This simple unit of interpersonal communication is the basis of self-esteem. We tend to note and to increase our acts that elicit rewarding responses; those actions producing undesired responses are used less and less frequently. To a large extent, the ratio of satisfactory to unsatisfactory responses is the index of our self-esteem.

Many responses from others are not easily interpreted as clear approval or disapproval. Most of us who are parents set an impossible task for ourselves: we want our children to believe that we love them unconditionally—without reservation; we also want them to behave in a reasonably acceptable way. To accomplish this we must respond approvingly to some of their behavior and disapprovingly to other actions. This will be communicated to them as *approving of them as persons* some of the time, and *disapproving of them as persons* at other times. For a child to interpret our responses as unconditional acceptance of him is almost impossible; therefore, our love will be viewed as conditional. A child learns that certain of his behavior is acceptable and some is not; he will learn to like parts of himself, and parts he will not. His self-esteem will reflect the amount of himself that he likes or accepts; to increase self-esteem he will tend to repress those parts of himself which he does not like.

Interpersonal communication is the hinge upon which this process swings. If a child cannot distinguish between (1) strong approval of himself (and his potential) and (2) disapproval of a few specific behaviors, then his self-esteem will not be congruent with the attitudes expressed by his parents and others toward him. Accurate communication of approval and disapproval of him is imperative to his appropriate development of self-esteem.

The maintenance of self-esteem is as important and complex as its development. Many of our attempts at maintenance are successful; some are self-defeating. *We should look first at those which are least likely to be successful because they are used altogether too much.*

There are three self-defeating approaches to maintenance of self-esteem: (1) trying to hide parts of ourselves from others, (2) acting as if we were something we are not, and (3) following only the "straight and narrow" ritualized patterns of interaction. Our interest in this discussion will center upon the ways in which interpersonal communication is related to the success or failure of such attempts; improving one's own communication habits through new insights should be the reader's goal.

When we perceive that parts of ourselves are eliciting disapproval, we may attempt to hide those parts—if we think it can be done. We then relate to others as "part-persons" rather than whole persons. For example, we may attempt to hide our anger when aroused. Or we may attempt to show no fear except when we are alone. Generally such attempts are ineffective: people usually see nonverbal signs of tension which are beyond our control; these are communicated to persons close to us despite our efforts to "say nothing." However, there are two considerations which are very important when we are successful at hiding such parts of ourselves. The first is that our anger or fear is stored up inside us, possibly influencing our later responses to communication from others. These feelings may break out in ways we don't understand and which are not understood by others. Such "breakouts" (or outbreaks") may not even be perceived by us but are easily seen by others.[18] In this fashion, later communication not related to the focus of our anger or fear may be influenced in such a way that others (and we) are confused. At best, such internalized anger and fear contribute to our problem of fighting off an early ulcer.[19] Improved habits of being open and frank in our interpersonal communication can be personally helpful.

A second possibly damaging effect of hiding parts of ourselves is that we cause apprehension in those persons with whom we relate. Suppose as your employer, I must tell you that you have failed to do your job in an adequate manner; suppose I tell you, and you show no reaction—you smile, remain calm, say nothing, and go your way. My interpretation is that you are a cool one, that you maintain your calmness through stiff self-discipline, and do not easily go out of control. But I also wonder if you'll "lay low and stab me in the back" when I'm not expecting it—I become suspicious of you! I wonder how many emotional stimuli you can take before you react; do you

18Rogers, *op. cit.*, pp. 338–346.
19S. Jourard, *The Transparent Self*, New York, Van Nostrand Reinhold, 1964 pp. 184–185.

remain calm under stress until at a certain point you "break" and cannot be depended upon at all? The point is this: you have given me no way to assess your emotional behavior—I perceive only part of you and suspect there is more. I have experienced you as only a "part-person," and as such you do not seem to be real. I am confused and will be suspicious until I learn more about you. In the meantime, this attitude will tend to distort my perceptions of even your ordinary, everyday communications which may be totally unrelated to the earlier event. In such fashion interpersonal communications and personal relationships are distorted by attempts to hide part of ourselves.

A second ineffective approach to maintaining our self-esteem is to pretend that we are something we are not. This approach includes attempts to communicate false messages about ourselves—to wear masks or to erect facades. This game can be carried to incredible extremes; we can even put forth a little of that part of ourselves which produces undesired responses and then deride, derogate, or castigate such behavior! Erving Goffman has carefully analyzed such forms of pretense in his book, The Presentation of Self in Everyday Life.[20] He draws a distinction between "expressions given" (genuine communication) and "expressions given off" (artificial communication) and cites a most insightful and humorous example taken from a novel by William Sansom in which Preedy, a vacationing Englishman, makes his first appearance on the beach at a summer resort:

> But in any case he took care to avoid catching anyone's eye. First of all, he had to make it clear to those potential companions of his holiday that they were of no concern to him whatsoever. He stared through them, round them, over them—eyes lost in space. The beach might have been empty. If by chance a ball was thrown his way, he looked surprised; then let a smile of amusement lighten his face [Kindly Preedy], looked around dazed to see that there were people on the beach, tossed it back with a smile to himself and not a smile at the people, and then resumed carelessly his nonchalant survey of space.

[20]E. Goffman, The Presentation of Self in Everyday Life, Garden City, N.Y., Doubleday Anchor, 1959.

*But it was time to institute a little parade of the Ideal Preedy. By devious handlings he gave any who wanted to look a chance to see the title of his book—a Spanish translation of Homer, classic thus, but not daring, cosmopolitan too—and then gathered together his beach-wrap and bag into a neat sand-resistant pile [Methodological and Sensible Preedy], rose slowly to stretch at ease his huge frame [Big-Cat Preedy], and tossed aside his sandals [Carefree Preedy after all].*

*The marriage of Preedy and the sea! There were alternative rituals. The first involved the stroll that turns into a run and a dive straight into the water, thereafter smoothing into a strong splashless crawl towards the horizon, but of course not really to the horizon. Quite suddenly he would turn on his back and thrash great white splashes with his legs, somehow thus showing that he could have swum further had he wanted to, and then stand up a quarter out of water for all to see who it was.*

*The alternative course was simpler, it avoided the cold-water shock and it avoided the risk of appearing too high-spirited. The point was to appear to be so used to the sea, the Mediterranean, and this particular beach, that one might as well be in the sea as out of it. It involved a stroll down and into the edge of the water—not even noticing his toes were wet, land and water all the same to him!—with his eyes up at the sky gravely surveying portents, invisible to others, of the weather [Local Fisherman Preedy].*[21]

It is quite possible for most of us to recall times when we have behaved in a manner somewhat similar to Preedy. We all play roles of one kind or another at various times. The important thing is to know when we are doing it, and to note the relative portion of our time devoted to such behavior. Are we ever ourselves?

A number of points may be made about pretending to be what we are not. In the first place, it takes much energy and concentration—while focusing on our performance, we may miss many

---

[21]W. Sansom, *A Contest of Ladies*, London, Hogarth, 1956, pp. 230–232.

clues to the way people are perceiving us. Goffman makes the point that many times people eventually discover that nobody is really watching these performances and in reality could not care less.[22] Such performances, when ignored, can amount to a severe loss of time and effort—time during which a genuinely rewarding interpersonal relationship might have been achieved.

In the second place, such play-acting must be good. Many a television comedy is based upon a character's pretense to be something he is not, with himself being the only member of the group who does not know that all others see through his facade. We may laugh at a comic character in a play, but we hardly want people laughing at our silly performance in real life. We'll mention more damaging effects later, but it seems bad enough to have people meet us and go away saying to themselves, "What an ass!"

A more damaging effect of another person's penetration of our "cover" is that he cannot further depend upon anything we do or say—suspicion haunts his every observation of our behavior— "What a phony!" He may never give us a very *obvious* clue of this suspicion, while his *subtle* show of a clue is lost by us in our concentration on our "performance." But when we need his confidence most—when we very much want his real trust and accurate estimate of our potential, when we ask him sincerely to give us a try—he will try others first, and we may be left alone with our pretenses, a lonely phony.

In our estimation, the most severe consequence of pretending to be something we are not is that it becomes a way of life. The more we pretend, the better we become at "playing a part." And the better we are at "playing parts," the more we will try to solve our problems of interpersonal relations *by pretense* rather than by honestly facing issues and working out solutions based upon reality. One phony bit of behavior thus produces another, and even if we convince many other people, we will be faced with the problem of trying to find our real self. "Who are you?" is the basic question asked of persons thought to be mentally disturbed. Unlimited pursuit of pretense in life can produce the seeds of madness.[23]

[22]Goffman, The Presentation of Self, op. cit., pp. 4–5.
[23]H. Deutsch, "The Imposter: Contribution to Ego Psychology of a Type of Psychopath," Psychoanalytical Quarterly, 24 (1955), 483–505.

The final disadvantage of pretense which will be mentioned here is that it seldom works for most people. Most of us are incapable of carrying it off on the nonverbal level. By tone of voice, facial expression, modified posture, jerkiness of gesture, and other elements of metacommunication usually beyond our control, we signal our anger, grief, fear, surprise, elation, and other real feelings and attitudes.[24] Few of us are adept at maintaining "poker faces" in our interactions. People may tolerate our pretense but they usually know it for what it is if they care at all to look. How, for example, would you be able to carry off a pretense which would deny the messages described below:

> In a sheltered corner of the room we stopped dancing
> altogether and talked, and what I distinctly remember is
> how her hands, beneath steady and opaque appraisal of
> her eyes, in nervous slurred agitation blindly sought mine
> and seized and softly gripped, with infantile instinct, my
> thumbs. Just my thumbs she held, and as we talked she moved
> them this way and that as if she were steering me. When
> I closed my eyes, the red darkness inside my lids was
> trembling, and when I rejoined my wife, and held her
> to dance, she asked, "Why are you panting?"[25]

A third ineffective approach to the maintenance of self-esteem is to be very cautious, to pursue only the ritualized, common, "tried and true" forms of interpersonal behavior. "I can't receive negative feedback if I only do as everybody else does." This process is one of deliberate hiding of unique parts of ourselves, responding to the fear that they may be discovered. The effect on the other person is one of appraising you as only a "part-person"—too cautious, unnatural, and somewhat unreal. In some cases the other person becomes somewhat apprehensive, wondering when your real self may show and what it will be like—and to what extent it may prove to be a threat.[26]

All three ineffective approaches to maintaining self-esteem

[24]P. Watzlawick, J. H. Beavin, and D. D. Jackson, *Pragmatics of Communication*, New York, Norton, 1967, pp. 62–67.
[25]J. Updike, *Pigeon Feathers*, New York, Crest Books, 1953, p. 176.
[26]Goffman, "On Face-Work;" *op. cit.*, 213–231.

discussed, hiding, pretending, and cautious adherence to ritualized responses, have been shown in one way or another to be a sham— unnatural, artificial, and to some extent damaging to our interpersonal interactions. Some of the time we may fool other people, and to some extent they may even succeed in helping us to fool ourselves. These approaches project a view of life which is superficial and lacking as to solid foundations, and thus ineffective in maintaining genuine self-esteem. The basis of a strong self-image is eroded.

Effective *maintenance* of self-esteem requires the same kind of behavior that developed it in the first place—exposure, feedback, and honest attempts at desirable change. The cycle must constantly be repeated. Maintaining self-esteem is a lifelong concern for most of us. Few persons appear to receive complete confirmation of perfection. As we expose new parts of ourselves and gain feedback, we see additional need to change; as we try to change, we receive new feedback evaluating these attempted changes. Thus, new exposures produce new change attempts, and so on as the cycle continues.

There can be no guarantee of continued self-esteem as we attempt new changes. We must risk our self-esteem with each attempt to improve it. Our doubts about our self-worth can only be dissipated by putting them to the test of self-exposure and feedback. In the long run, probably the best type of self-esteem is confidence in our ability to use this approach—*confidence that we can maintain our self-esteem by using self-exposure and feedback.*

This procedure involves exposure of ourselves through initiating (usually) communication or sometimes by responding to communication of others. It also involves *evaluative feedback*. By evaluative feedback we mean reflected appraisals of ourselves as exposed. These are useful for self-evaluation and making decisions to attempt self-change. Persons with excessive fears and very low self-esteem will be able to accept only feedback which is reassuring. Those with higher self-esteem can risk the acceptance of feedback which shows some weaknesses or unacceptable aspects of themselves. They can test their assumptions about their real worth, acceptability, lovability, and value to other persons.

There are two general classes of communication feedback useful for evaluating self-worth. When people communicate, however impersonally, they give off very subtle cues. We call this *indirect* feedback. *Direct* feedback consists of verbal statements explicitly describing one person's reactions to another.

Indirect feedback is often ambiguous. A smile may be a polite social habit. Aloofness may indicate disapproval or it *may* indicate the *other person's fear* of his self-exposure and consequent evaluation. The problem is magnified by a person's tendency to see what he expects to see, to be sensitive to those cues which confirm his expectations.[27] Thus, if we are suspicious of our self-worth, we are more likely to note cues which confirm our suspicions.[28]

Indirect feedback tends to be overgeneralized. It is frequently difficult to associate our feeling of rejection by another person with any one of our own specific acts. We tend to experience such rejection of some minor part of our behavior as rejection of our whole self, or all parts of ourselves about which we have doubts. Indirect feedback does not provide for explanation, specificity, or justification. In addition, indirect feedback may reveal more about the other person than about us—consequently, when we are very fearful, we can rationalize a negative response from another person by attributing it to their weakness, injustice, narrowness, or to deliberate malice.[29] Such indirect feedback is not very useful and may easily be misinterpreted. Be careful of generalizing about yourself on the basis of indirect feedback.

Direct feedback is potentially more useful for evaluating self-worth; however, it is useless, even harmful, if it is not frank and honest. Frank evaluations are difficult to obtain because of our cultural taboos. We tend to approve people who look for and respond to "some good in everyone." We think it is somehow wrong to look critically at and to speak openly to another person. Maslow has noted that even our definitions of love do not ordinarily include an obligation to give open and honest interpersonal evaluation; he points out the irony of our willingness to let someone go on doing damage

[27]M. Deutsch and L. Solomon, "Reactions to Evaluations by Others as Influenced by Self-Evaluations," *Sociometry, 22* (1959), 93–112.
[28]J. W. Thibaut and H. W. Riecken, "Some Determinants and Consequences of the Perception of Social Causality," *Journal of Personality, 24* (1955), 113–133.
[29]F. Heider, *The Psychology of Interpersonal Relations, op. cit.,* pp. 169–173.

to himself and others, *ostensibly out of kindness!*[30] Probably our own fear of hurting someone and receiving retaliation is our real motivation.[31] Requesting frank and honest evaluation of us from another person will require courage; however, it can be of great value if used for purposes of self-improvement.

## The Facilitation of Personal Change

Increasing self-esteem requires positive reevaluation of oneself. This reevaluation requires exposure plus awareness and honest responses on the part of another person. As pointed out, it is very difficult for a person to achieve change in interpersonal behavior without interaction with other persons.[32] The helpful relationship is one in which there is unconditional acceptance of a person (or his potential) combined with honest, direct feedback. Some persons achieve this relationship. It begins when people trust themselves and each other enough to start exposing more and more of their thoughts, ideas, and feelings. Each exposure is tentative; it comes in small increments and the response is noted. A disapproving response may stop the interaction temporarily or even permanently. When exposures are met with acceptance, interpersonal trust and self-confidence start to build. Each interracting party is mutually reinforcing: when one person trusts enough to expose himself more, trust is generated in the other person.[33]

In order to establish a relationship in which interpersonal communication of this order can be achieved, we may have to go out of our way to find persons who are open and frank and accepting toward us. There is increasing evidence that such relationships can be obtained if sought, with consequent benefit to both of the interacting persons.[34] Such relationships are to be prized and protected with great care and caring.

---

[30]A. H. Maslow, "Summer Notes on Social Psychology of Industry and Management," Non-Linear Systems, Inc., Del Mar, California, unpublished manuscript, 1962.

[31]W. G. Bennis, et al., *Interpersonal Dynamics*, rev. ed., Homewood, Ill., Dorsey, 1968, pp. 35–39.

[32]*Ibid.*, pp. 505–523.

[33]J. Gibb, "Defensive Communication," *Journal of Communication, 11* (1961), 141–148.

[34]D. Barnlund, *Interpersonal Communication*, Boston, Houghton Mifflin, 1968, pp. 613–645.

We have given extensive consideration to the development of self-image and the achievement of self-esteem. We have done so deliberately because, in all of the areas in which interpersonal communication influences people, we can think of nothing which is more important. We believe that these elements are fundamental to most if not all human interaction.

## PERSONAL ENJOYMENT VIA COMMUNICATION

We have suggested in the previous section that one objective of interpersonal communication is that of personal development. A second, and closely related, value of interaction is simply personal enjoyment.

### The Pleasure of Shared Personal Growth

When a person has a good self-image, when his self-esteem is reasonably secure, he can greatly enjoy communicating with others. Interpersonal exchange is then exhilarating: ideas bounce back and forth; response and feedback are openly given and easily accepted. The pleasure lies in the interaction, not simply in telling or just in listening. When such an instance occurs we are struck by the feeling, "Isn't he (or she) a wonderful person?" Such experiences actually are wonderful.

There can be a certain pleasure in exposing some of our more protected thoughts and feelings to trusted others. We take pleasure in articulating such thoughts; some of them may have been little understood by us until we started to express them, and they may take shape in ways we had not quite planned or even suspected. There is pleasure in having such thoughts and feelings become clearer as we gain honest feedback. Sometimes we feel that they must be reassessed or reshaped by us; sometimes we achieve solid confirmation from other persons.

There is also pleasure in seeing this happen to the other person, joy in participating in his personal growth and development. There is gratification in giving honest feedback when you feel it will not be misused. It is our belief that most families would like to have such a relationship, and that interpersonal communication of this order between parents and children would make parenthood worthy of the name.

### The Pleasure of Shared Silence

When personal growth and development have been shared and enjoyed, frequently moments of silent communion are the result. In such cases interpersonal communication has not stopped; the persons so involved are quite aware of each other's presence and feelings. There is an atmosphere of shared trust and confidence, one in which one's own feelings are secure and one's feelings about the other person are also secure. There is also a willing tolerance of the other person's need for silence, with security in knowing that their thoughts will give them pleasure. There is a ready willingness to offer independence to the other person—freedom to think as he wishes, to develop thoughts and feelings which may be shared at some future time or perhaps never shared.

Such nonverbal interpersonal communion is usually very restful, frequently much more so than merely being alone. Occasionally an autobiography or diary will attest the value of such moments. Our own personal experiences corroborate this principle. Sometimes there was an environmental element, such as a sunset or the shadows creeping along the basin of the valley below. Sometimes such conditions seemed to offer an excuse to enjoy shared silence. But the thing that was later recalled with greatest pleasure was not the sunset or the valley—but the restful comfort of the moment of silence enjoyed together. Such moments of silent communion provide a yardstick by which to judge the quality of an interpersonal relationship.

### The Value of Phatic Communion

We have discussed the value of shared silence; a similar kind of communion occurs when people make pleasant noises at each other. The emotional feeling is not nearly so deep, but the pleasure is genuine.

The purpose of much "small talk" is to acknowledge in a pleasant way the presence of another person. Commonly used greetings and idle chatter are illustrations of a type of communication which has been labeled *phatic communion*.[35] We use such pleasant noises to signal that we welcome interaction, that we are friendly, or that we at least recognize the presence of the other person. In English such courtesies tend to be rather unimaginative: "Hello," "Nice day," "Howdy," "Hi." We call these greetings "noises" because no literal meaning is usually intended. If someone asks, "How are you?" they would indeed be surprised by even a brief medical report, however accurate. A precise response could be humorous, as when James Thurber was once asked, "How's your wife?" and he replied, "Compared to what?"

A simple illustration of the nature of phatic communion is the story of an American businessman traveling in Europe. At lunch he found himself seated across from a Frenchman whose language he did not speak. Each smiled a greeting. As the wine was served, the Frenchman raised his glass and said, "Bon appetit." The American, wanting to be friendly, replied, "Ginsberg." That evening at dinner the exact procedure occurred again. The waiter noticed this peculiar exchange and after dinner called the American aside to explain that the Frenchman was not giving his name but saying that he "hopes you enjoy your meal." The following day the American sought out the Frenchman at lunch, hoping to correct his error. At his first opportunity the American raised his glass and said, "Bon appetit!" to which the Frenchman proudly replied, "Ginsberg!" This story was told to the students in one of our class lectures. For days when occasionally meeting one of those students in the hall we could expect a joyful smile, an upraised hand, and an enthusiastic, "Ginsberg." The greeting actually served us much better than a linguistically meaningful, "I'm happy to see you."

In comparing the deeply emotional value of silent communion with the casual use of phatic communion, it may seem incongruous to note any relationship. The only point we will try to make is that without the small talk first there can be little important talk later. Silence between two people cannot be expected to be shared communion unless it is preceded by small talk, further exposure, honest feedback, and increased trust, plus shared discovery and growth.

[35]B. Malinowski, "The Problem of Meaning in Primitive Languages," Supplement I in C. K. Ogden and I. A. Richards, *The Meaning of Meaning*, New York, Harcourt, Brace & World, 1923, pp. 296–336.

Otherwise, the silence likely will just be silence, sometimes filled with loneliness, occasional signs of tension, and the possibility of emergent hostility. In starting down the path of improving interpersonal relations, we have to start somewhere; one good beginning is the cordial use of phatic communion.

## The Pleasure of Shared Noise

An enjoyable form of communication upon which little research has been done is the enjoyment of shared noise. We are not referring here to sounds used as signals or symbols, such as factory whistles signifying time to quit work, but the pleasure derived from shared noises for the sake of enjoyment alone.

It is common knowledge that babies babble, gurgle, and coo. There is evidence that they do it more when they are happy (or are happier when they do it). In living with teen-agers in one's family it soon becomes quite clear that noise unshared is noise not enjoyed; in fact, it seems that the more persons with whom it is shared, the more the teen-type pleasure. Teenie-boppers produce nonlinguistic squeals, squawks, and squalls; they appear to enjoy sharing these verbal gymnastics with each other.

Persons of all ages tend to enjoy sharing rhythmic and melodious sound. We need not discuss the joy of sharing the sound of music; however, the shared sound of litanies in worship and the use of ritual in patriotic ceremonies have something in common. Parents soon discover their own pleasure as well as that of their children in hearing stories read aloud.

We have yet to assess the full and lasting value of the effects of psychedelic color joined with strange, bombastic, and compelling sounds; however, there is wide acceptance of the idea that a very interesting and pleasurable form of interpersonal communication is simply that of sharing nonlinguistic sounds with persons whose company you enjoy.

## FULFILLING SOCIAL EXPECTATIONS

The individual uses interpersonal communication to meet his need for fulfilling social expectations. In almost all cultures the individual is expected to comply with a minimal number of these social requirements.

## Acknowledging the Presence of Others

In our culture this expectation is usually met by a simple "Hello" or "How are you?" As we have noted in our discussion of such phatic communication, the linguistic content of such messages is usually insignificant, but the message communicated is quite important. Studies have shown that simple failure to acknowledge a person's presence is painful if not insulting; few persons find comfort in situations which lack sociability.[36] The democratic act of social recognition may appear to be somewhat perfunctory or even artificial, but is the action of individuals who desire to create little moments of pleasurable interaction, moments when the stresses of life are temporarily set aside and two persons may simply enjoy being together on a friendly basis. Such brief encounters are very important to an individual's psychological well-being and enjoyment of life.

In acknowledging the presence of others, nonlinguistic behavior carries the weight of the communication: a pleasant vocal tone accompanied by a friendly facial expression fulfills a person's expectation of acknowledgment of his presence. In large part the nonverbal behavior actually sets the tone of the encounter. What is said is of less importance than the manner in which it is presented.

## Acknowledging the Nature of a Social Situation

There are two very important elements in a social situation which, if not agreed upon by the participants, can cause considerable confusion, frustration, and disgust. The first is the purpose of the encounter or meeting; the second is the role-function of each participant.

Preliminary identification of the purpose of a meeting between two or more persons can expose any difference in viewpoints and diminish possible misunderstanding; in this way early agreement on the purpose of the interaction can facilitate further communication.

Acknowledgment of participant roles is equally important; the role of an expert source of relevant information, or the role of a

[36]H. D. Duncan, *Communication and Social Order*, New York, Oxford Univ. Press, 1962, pp. 20–24.

group member who holds power over others, needs to be identified if the interaction is to be optimally functional. Misunderstanding or disagreement on such roles can produce confusion and endless bickering. Considerable research has been done on the relationship between roles and interpersonal communication; a person fulfilling the requirements of a role as he comprehends it is easily disturbed if his behavior is perceived as inappropriate.

Roles as such are neither right nor wrong, but may be inadequately understood by the person attempting to fulfill a role or by his perceivers. Roles as such may be more or less explicit and more or less crucial; however, a role "violation" is no more than the violation of an assumption either on the part of the role-player or his associates.[37] A homely illustration of communication difficulty is that of a university official who considers himself to be responsible for the moral principles adhered to by the student body, when the students consider him to be responsible only for selection of staff and review of curricular offerings. Such disagreement regarding role, if unidentified, can cause considerable confusion and interpersonal antagonism. Clarification of role perceptions would at least identify the primary source of disagreement.

### Clarifying the Nature of a Relationship with Another Person

It is easy to see that given a little time a person can change. Because of new or different experiences or associations with others, he can change in terms of expertness as to some particular operation or principle, or in degree of power or social influence, or in the nature of his own self-image. We were recently exposed to the concept of the "New Mr. Nixon" as compared to the "Old Nixon."

When former associates meet following a period of separation, it is quite important to reaffirm the previous relationship before continuing interaction. An assumption that a prior relationship is still in effect is inappropriate; a brief exploration of how the relationship currently is viewed can expose new and different perceptions or indicate that the old basis is a solid one, still in effect. Businessmen

---

[37]For recent surveys of research on the function of roles in human interaction see B. J. Biddle and E. J. Thomas, *Role Theory: Concepts and Research,* New York, Wiley, 1966, and E. J. Thomas and R. A. Feldman, *Concepts of Role Theory,* Ann Arbor, Mich., Univ. of Michigan Press, 1964.

seem to find this procedure a bit awkward; however, teen-agers in love seem to make it a daily occurrence—in fact, sometimes they seem to do little else as they interact with each other.

This problem is particularly pertinent to a leader-follower relationship. People in authority roles (for example, parents) seem to take for granted that a relationship with a subordinate will never change; such an assumption holds real danger in terms of interpersonal cooperation and personal satisfaction. An authority relationship needs to be reaffirmed periodically if the relationship is to be functionally effective.

Predictable changes in a relationship need to be identified and affirmed. Such a situation is the new relationship between a husband and wife at the birth of their first child. Probable changes in such a relationship need to be explored, mutual agreement and understanding need to be achieved, and reaffirmed periodically as social conditions change (for example, as the baby becomes a young child, etc.).

To reaffirm a prior relationship is simply to fulfill a social expectation; a mutually agreeable relationship is easily renewed. On the other hand, if events have transpired calling for a new relationship, the participants logically should start interaction with a discussion of required changes in their mode of interacting with each other.

### Complying with Cultural Norms

Different cultures have developed different norms of human interaction. Typically these are minor variations, but they are sometimes quite noticeable when one meets a representative from another culture.

For a well-educated, well-traveled person, accommodation of such differences is not difficult; the point to be made here is that such accommodation needs to occur and genuinely facilitates interpersonal communication.

There appear to be three general categories of cultural differences in communication according to Edward T. Hall: formal customs, informal customs, and technological communication patterns.[38] Formal communication customs of a culture are overt and easily identified by an observer; they include forms of address indicating acknowl-

[38]E. T. Hall, The Silent Language, New York, Doubleday, 1959, pp. 9–13.

edgment of differences in status, protocol regarding who may be addressed by whom, when and where a status person may or must be acknowledged, and appropriate methods of bargaining in the marketplace. For example, to an Arab, bargaining is not only a pleasant way of passing time, it is actually a formal technique for interpersonal relations.

Informal communication customs are covert, subtle, and frequently difficult to identify. They are implicit rather than explicit, and are deeply imbedded in the subconscious. However, they are extremely important and seriously influence the relationship between members of different cultures. An excellent example is a cultural attitude toward the passage of time. In America we consider time to be a very valuable commodity, even if we are seeking to use it for purposes of relaxation. Many a vacationing American tourist has had moments of severe frustration when faced with a different attitude toward time on the part of a Latin-American innkeeper. Other significant informal norms in American culture are the following: (1) an implicit assumption that hard work will be rewarded; (2) a tendency to see things in bipolar opposites—black and white, good or bad, old or new; (3) little emphasis on tradition and great emphasis on that which is new; (4) high regard for technological change; and (5) general rejection of a show of one's emotions.

Despite the American's general rejection of emotional display, deep emotions are invested in these informal cultural factors. Part of the success of noted trial lawyers is their ability to provide stimuli which appeal to informal cultural patterns on the part of juries. The late Clarence Darrow dressed himself in an old sloppy suit; he appealed to the common man's instincts—people could identify with him—he was their type, "the country realist who can outsmart a dishonest city slicker." He realized that many people do not know the law but have a deep sense of informal justice and will even weep where they see homely justice outraged. This was Darrow's strength, and the only time he really failed to capitalize on it was when he was called to Honolulu for the Massie Case in 1932; there he faced a jury with a different sense of informal justice—the Chinese jurors failed to be moved by his American culture-rooted strategies.

Anxiety is easily aroused when a cultural norm is unexpectedly breached, for example, premature use of a first name. What happens next depends upon the existing cultural norms for handling anxiety; the American culture pattern is one of withdrawal and calm reserve—in Japan men giggle or laugh nervously. These cultural modes for handling anxiety are nearly automatic and relatively restricted; in fact, the leeway provided for different emotional responses is less than one might think. And the real problem arises when one tries to respond properly to an emotional response of someone from another culture. The point is this: norms for emotional responses to emotional behavior are learned informally and people seldom realize that they have been learned at all—they tend to think that their cultural norm is the only proper, reasonable way to behave. This whole matter of deviation from informal emotional norms bristles with complexity; however, it has immediate impact on the effectiveness of interpersonal communication between persons of different cultures.

The third class of cultural differences, technological communication patterns, are generally specific, readily talked about, and more easily transmitted to persons of other cultures. Technological communication is fully conscious behavior. It is usually quite explicit and frequently written down and recorded; it is also usually characterized by suppression of personal feelings, since they tend to interfere with functional operations of personnel, machines, and material. Actually, personal feelings tend to reflect informal social norms which are difficult to make explicit, and thus make transmission of technical information more difficult; hence, informal social norms are played down. When American technicians work in another culture they try to help people help themselves and not run afoul of the local formal and informal social norms. Changes are introduced in those parts of the lives of the local people *which are treated technically,* such as in the cases of transportation or public health measures. Such technical changes are readily observed, talked about, and transmitted to others. In such fashion entire armies from different cultures can collaborate on a military objective; political collaboration, on the other hand, heavily involves informal social norms, such as who sits side by side at a conference table; and cultural differences in such informal communication patterns may disrupt, if not completely eliminate, collaboration between people of different cultures—witness the problems of the conferees regarding negotiations in the Vietnamese war.

Compliance with cultural norms—formal, informal, and technical—is a very important use of interpersonal communication in order to fulfill social expectations. Such social expectations can frequently be influenced by the larger social environment—a continent, a nation, or a race; they are, of course, heavily influenced, especially on the level of informal social customs, by local customs, subcultures and minority groups.

To summarize briefly, interpersonal communication is used to fulfill social expectations by acknowledging the presence of others, acknowledging the nature of a social situation, clarifying the nature of a relationship with another person, and complying with cultural norms in a given situation. Each of these ways of fulfilling social expectations through interpersonal communication may seriously affect the relationships between people and the benefits to be derived from such relationships.

## NEGOTIATING WITH OTHERS

In previous sections of this chapter we have indicated that an individual uses interpersonal communication to meet his needs for personal development and personal enjoyment, and for fulfilling social expectations. A fourth way in which interpersonal communication helps to meet one's needs is that of negotiating with other people.

### A Mixed-Motive Situation

There are many interpersonal situations in which the two (or more) persons involved are not entirely cooperative. More often than not the goal of one or another individual contains both cooperative and competitive motivation. For example, suppose your car will not start on a cold morning; the relationship between you as owner and a mechanic as repairman is both cooperative and competitive. Both of you can benefit from negotiating an agreement in which he earns a fee and you achieve an auto which functions in cold weather—to this extent both of your motivations are cooperative. On the other hand, the terms of the agreement are competitive—the higher the mechanic's fee, the greater the relative value to him; conversely, the lower the fee, the greater the relative value to you (assuming the quality of his workmanship remains the same). Such interpersonal situations have been studied under the label of "mixed-motive negotiations." Many interpersonal relationships fall into this category.

The study of such negotiation or bargaining relationships has usually focused upon two questions: (1) for a specified set of conditions, what procedures are likely to be used by the participants, and (2) what decision will likely be the outcome? The theory of negotiated games has been used to find answers to these questions.[39]

## Application of Game Theory to Mixed-Motive Situations

Game theory as applied to negotiation situations rests on the assumption that individuals attempt to achieve the highest possible returns (in terms of each individual's value system) by interacting with others. On the basis of this assumption Nash[40] has developed a formula for the probable outcome of a mixed-motive interaction; it defines a solution which maximizes the net (combined) returns to both participants.[41] This formula has been found useful in predicting outcomes of negotiations when each participant's outcome values can be measured or estimated accurately; the problem of measurement of "utility preferences" has given rise to a large, important, and highly technical literature in the past fifteen or twenty years, much of which is known as "utility theory."[42]

## Role of Communication in Mixed-Motive Situations

If the theory of negotiated games is to provide insight into mixed-motive interactions, communication between the participants must be considered; in very recent research, direct verbal communication has been studied as a part of the negotiation process. A re-

[39]For an introductory treatment of game theory see A. Rapoport, *Two Person Game Theory: The Essential Ideas,* Ann Arbor, Mich., Univ. of Michigan Press, 1966.
[40]J. Nash, "The Bargaining Problem," *Econometrica, 18* (1950), 155–162.
[41]Nash's formula identifies the predicted outcome to a mixed-motive situation as that solution which maximizes the value of the expression $(U_1 (A_J) - U_1 (C))$ $(U_2 (A_J) - U_2 (C))$ where $U_1 (A_J)$ is the utility attached to alternative $A_J$ by the *ith* participant and $U_1 (C)$ is the utility attached to the condition of conflict by that participant.
[42]For a good introduction to utility theory see J. Marshak, "Scaling of Utilities and Probability," in M. Shubik, ed., *Game Theory and Related Approaches to Social Behavior,* New York, Wiley, 1964, pp. 95–101.

search effort by Beisecker[43] has explored the role of communication in mixed-motive negotiations.

Beisecker has concluded that the potential impact of communication on the outcome of a negotiation is related to the degree that each participant initially can estimate the other's position. When participants have only limited knowledge of each other's utility values, or when these tend to change during interaction, understanding of such values can be achieved only with the aid of communication; estimates will tend to be valid to the extent that such communication is effective.

Beisecker has also developed a theoretical analysis of the ways in which communication can aid participants in pursuit of both cooperative and competitive goals.[44] Communication can be employed cooperatively by two or more persons to produce a group decision which gives maximum satisfaction to all participants. The role of cooperative communication is to discover and increase areas of common interest; it provides a search process through which the participants identify previously unnoticed alternatives, reconsider criteria for evaluating alternatives, and strive for greater logical consistency among their utility (evaluative) systems. Most scholars who study this process have labeled it "problem-solving" discussion or interaction. Communication also can be employed competitively to distort the other person's perceptions of the situation in order to gain an individual bargaining advantage. Strategies for accomplishing this are numerous, including the following: (1) misrepresentation of available alternatives, (2) misrepresentation of utility (value) of various alternatives, (3) rejection of additional alternatives, (4) rejection of additional criteria for estimating utilities of alternatives, (5) insisting on the other person's need to achieve an agreement, and (6) indicating high commitment to a demand for resolution. There are additional strategies that could be identified; however, in each case the purpose is to alter the other person's perception of the outcome when a specific agreement is reached. Mothers and sometimes fathers seem to be altogether

---

[43]T. Beisecker, "The Use of Persuasive Strategies in Dyadic Interaction," unpublished Ph.D. dissertation, Univ. of Wisconsin, 1968.

[44]T. Beisecker, "The Role of Verbal Communication in Interpersonal Interaction; An Analysis from the Point of View of Games," Lawrence, Kan., Communication Research Center, Univ. of Kansas, 1969.

too adept at the use of these strategies in negotiating with their off-spring.[45]

In this discussion, it should be noticed that competitive communication strategies are here viewed (deliberately) as unjust or "unfair" when attempts are made to distort another person's perception of a situation or the value-system involved. On the other hand, a *mutual effort to search* for new alternatives, new value systems, or greater internal consistency may produce differences of opinion, but such *efforts toward accurate or objective perception of a bargaining situation* are just and fair, and can be viewed broadly as a cooperative effort.

In our culture, deliberate distortion of the perceptions of another person is unethical. However, from time to time one may find it practiced; if such were not the case there would be little need for such a discussion of "mixed-motive interaction." In many situations the participants possess simultaneous motivations both to be cooperative and to be competitive; sometimes one or the other is uppermost, and sometimes the individual himself would be hard pressed to analyze his interpersonal motivations objectively. In any case, *to provide an opportunity* for another person to alter his perceptions in a mutual search for a negotiated agreement is not unethical; however, *to distort deliberately* the perceptions of others is an irresponsible and unethical use of communication in an interpersonal situation.

Both cooperative and competitive communication can serve specific purposes in a mixed-motive situation by providing information needed by the participants. One of these purposes is to indicate to each other the utility values attached to each possible bargaining alternative; data can be given concerning such values and the firmness with which such is held. Procedurally this may take the form of one person offering to "settle" for certain considerations by the other, followed by the other person telling what he thinks of the offer.

A second purpose is served when each person indicates his perception of the interpersonal relationship between the participants: can the other person be trusted as a source of pertinent information (e.g., does he bluff); does he view himself as a subordinate or supe-

[45]For a very insightful and interesting analysis of parental competitive communication strategies see C. Russell and W. M. S. Russell, *Human Behaviour*, Boston, Little, Brown, pp. 189–247.

rior to the other; and is one person heavily dependent upon the other for needed information, or does he have access to a reliable "outside" source?

Finally, a useful purpose is served by discussion of the negotiation process itself: determination of an agenda, speaking order, speaker responsibilities, data desired, etc.

Much of the discussion above seems to imply that people mainly negotiate on matters of material value, and indeed much of the research on negotiation focuses upon this type of bargaining. However, it should be made perfectly clear that a large amount of interpersonal negotiation concerns matters less tangible, such as criteria for gaining personal regard, standards for determining status, procedures for showing recognition, and a host of other areas which require social contracts or agreements if people are to achieve personal satisfaction from their interaction with others. It is fairly safe to assume that almost anything is likely to have utility value for someone somewhere. If it has such value, one may have to negotiate with others in order for such value to be enjoyed.

## SUMMARY

In this chapter we have tried to identify those reasons why it is very important for a person to communicate personally and informally with other people. We have identified the following human needs or motivations: personal growth and development by achieving a desired self-image, fulfilling social expectations, and negotiating with others. Probably the personal need in which you are most interested and want the most information about concerns the attainment of a desirable self-image; in anticipation of this special interest we have dealt at some length with the search for self-identity, the social criteria for self-esteem, and the ways in which techniques of interpersonal communication can be used to facilitate your own change of behavior as you attempt to achieve greater personal self-esteem. We have placed special emphasis on the potential value of open, honest, and direct feedback from others concerning your own behavior. Some of the learning experiences suggested below are designed to provide such feedback; we urge you to follow these suggestions and to the best of your ability utilize the personal information thus obtained.

## Suggested Applications and Learning Experiences

1. With two or three of your closest friends discuss actual people you know who try to act as if they are smarter, better educated, or more experienced than they really are; after about twenty or thirty minutes, ask your friends to give you some feedback on whether or not they see you sometimes behaving in a similar way. Offer such feedback to them if they ask for it.

2. Attend a meeting of some campus problem-solving group, such as a planning group for a dormitory or house party; while you are participating in this group, as an experiment follow very carefully "straight and narrow" patterns which reflect generally "what everybody believes." After you have done this for one meeting, if one member of the group is a good friend tell him what you have been doing and how you plan to be different during the next meeting. Ask for his help and support during the next meeting as you attempt to do more than "just what everybody expects."

3. With two of your classmates write a three-person skit in which one "actor" presents only a small part of himself and the other "actors" try to obtain more information from him about himself. Ask your teacher if you may present this skit to the class. Have the class give you feedback on whether or not they know people who behave this way in real life and how they respond to such persons.

4. With a particularly good friend or helpful classmate mutually attempt to share some of your more protected thoughts and feelings about yourself. Strive especially for clarity as you try to express these thoughts and feelings. Listen very carefully to the responses the other person gives as you talk about yourself. Pay close attention to responses which indicate that some of your notions about yourself seem to be unwarranted. Discuss ways in which you can achieve growth and maturity by behaving differently. Note new perceptions of yourself as you begin to think about adopting some of these new behaviors.

5. Select some person of your acquaintance who represents a different culture or subculture, such as a foreign country or a ghetto area; ask that person to have lunch with you "to get better acquainted." Ask him to indicate ways in which your behavior (including especially your habitual communication patterns) are different from those customary in his culture. Have him tell you how he feels concerning these differences. Give him similar information if he asks for it.

6. Meet with one of your classmates and attempt to trade something you have (either a material item or services) for something he has. Note carefully any attempts on either his part or your part to distort each other's perceptions.

## Suggested Readings

*Berlo, David K., "Interaction," *The Process of Communication,* New York, Holt, Rinehart and Winston, 1960, pp. 106–131.

Festinger, Leon, "A Theory of Social Comparison Processes," *Human Relations, 7* (1954), 117–140.

*Giffin, Kim, and Heider, Mary, "The Relationship Between Speech Anxiety and the Suppression of Communication in Childhood," *Psychiatric Quarterly Supplement,* Part 2 (1967), 311–322.

Goffman, Erving, *The Presentation of Self in Everyday Life,* Garden City, N.Y., Doubleday Anchor, 1959, pp. 1–70.

Jourard, Sidney, *The Transparent Self,* New York, Van Nostrand Reinhold, pp. 9–30.

Rogers, Carl, *On Becoming a Person,* Boston, Houghton Mifflin, 1961, pp. 329–346.

*Schutz, William C., "The Postulate of Interpersonal Needs," *The Interpersonal Underworld,* Palo Alto, Calif., Science and Behavior Books, 1966, pp. 13–33.

---

*Items thus identified are reprinted in Kim Giffin and Bobby R. Patton, *Basic Readings in Interpersonal Communication,* New York, Harper & Row, 1971.

# interpersonal perception and communication | 3

The first step in communicating with another person is to form some impression of him. This impression directs our reactions to him and thus influences the course of interpersonal communication. This process of forming impressions of personality is called both "social perception" (when dealing solely with others) or more broadly "person perception" (which includes one's own self-perceptions).

Sociologists have long been interested in the special nature of interpersonal perception. Concepts of the two selves, the "I" and the "me,"[1] and a concern for the "looking-glass self,"[2] discussed in Chapter 2, have gained wide acceptance. Both theories point out that the child first develops an awareness of himself as a separate entity distinct from his environment because other people respond to him as a separate object. Without other people, then, we could have no self-concept. As we develop a concept of "self," we become aware of ourselves as objects of our own perceptions (the "me") apart and

[1] G. H. Mead, *Mind, Self and Society*, Chicago, Univ. of Chicago Press, 1934.
[2] C. H. Cooley, *Human Nature and the Social Order*, New York, Scribner's, 1902; 1922; 1930.

distinct from ourselves as perceivers (the "I"). Further, our evaluations of ourselves arise as a reflection of others' evaluations of us. Thus, the very heart of an individual's personality, his own self-concept, is believed to arise and develop through the process of social interaction.

The process of perception is generally believed to accomplish two things:

1. The individual recodes the diversity of data he encounters in a form simple enough to be retained by his limited memory; and
2. He mentally goes beyond the data given to predict future events, and thereby minimize surprise.[3]

These two accomplishments of perception, and selective recoding and prediction, become the basis for forming our impressions of other people. In forming our impression of another, we observe his actions and expressive movements, we notice his voice, we note what he says and does as he responds to us and other stimuli. From this data we make inferences about his cognitions, his needs, his emotions and feeling, his goals, and his attitudes. Our actions toward him and prediction of future interactions are guided by these judgments. Simultaneously the other person is making judgments about us that will direct his subsequent communications to us. If our judgments of one another are correct, genuine communication can be established and effective interaction becomes possible. If, however, our observations or predictions of one another are incorrect, communication is hampered and difficulties may develop in our interpersonal relations.

As with the other variables in the process of interpersonal communication, our person perceptions (that is, our perception of another's personality) are never static; we are constantly in a state of modification and reevaluation. The flawless boyfriend of last week may now be the most despicable villain of the twentieth century. As we have greater and more diverse opportunities for interaction, our perceptions undergo change. The two people in the divorce court are basically the same people who one day stood side by side at the altar—only now they know each other better.

[3]J. S. Bruner, "Social Psychology and Perception," in E. Maccoby, T. M. Newcomb, and E. L. Hartley, eds., *Readings in Social Psychology*, New York, Holt, Rinehart and Winston, 1958, pp. 85–94.

In this chapter we shall examine some of the factors that influence our impressions of one another and affect the foundation of our efforts to communicate.

## IMPRESSION FORMATION

A significant experiment by Solomon Asch attempted to determine how people form impressions of personality. The experimenter read to some college students a number of characteristics which were said to belong to an unknown person. For example, one list included such adjectives as "energetic," "assured," "cold," "inquisitive," "talkative," "ironical," and "persuasive." After the list was repeated a second time, the subjects were instructed to write a description of their impression of this person. One student wrote:

*He impresses people as being more capable than he really is. He is popular and never ill at ease. Easily becomes the center of attraction at any gathering. He is likely to be a jack-of-all-trades. Although his interests are varied, he is not necessarily well versed in any of them. He possesses a sense of humor. His presence stimulates enthusiasm and very often he does arrive at a position of importance.*

Another subject reported:

*He is the type of person you meet all too often: sure of himself, talks too much, always trying to bring you around to his way of thinking, and with not much feeling for the other fellow.*

Thus, the discrete terms on the list were organized into a single, unified personality. The subjects even gained impressions about characteristics not mentioned ("He possesses a sense of humor"). Asch summarized his study as follows:

*When a task of this kind is given, a normal adult is capable of responding to the instruction by forming a unified impression.*

*Though he hears a sequence of discrete terms, his resulting impression is not discrete.*[4]

The complexities and contradictions in people may be too great, however, to permit a unified impression to emerge. Another experiment involved a motion picture showing a young woman in five different scenes, designed to portray divergent aspects of her personality. In the first scene she is shown being "picked up" in front of a shabby hotel; in the second she is going to a bar with a man different from the one who had "picked her up"; the third scene shows her giving aid to a woman who has fallen down a public stairway; the fourth shows her giving money to a beggar; and the final scene shows her walking and talking with another young woman.

The film was shown to a group of college students, and they were asked to write their impression of the woman's personality. The investigators then divided the responses into three categories:

1. *Unified.* The major character qualities of sexual promiscuity and kindliness were able to be integrated by 23 percent of the respondents.
2. *Simplified.* Forty-eight percent of the subjects retained only one of the two major character qualities.
3. *Aggregated.* Twenty-nine percent of the subjects kept both major character qualities but failed to unify their impression.

Thus, less than a fourth of the students were able to achieve an organized impression of the divergent bits of information.[5]

The importance of first impressions in our interpersonal relationships was confirmed by a series of studies by social psychologist, Abraham S. Luchins. In one study Luchins composed two separate paragraphs about a person named Jim:

1. *Jim left the house to get some stationery. He walked out into the sun-filled street with two of his friends, basking in the sun as he walked. Jim entered the stationery store, which was full of people. Jim talked with an acquaintance while he*

[4]S. E. Asch, "Forming Impressions of Personality," *Journal of Abnormal and Social Psychology,* 41 (1946), 258–290.
[5]E. S. Gollin, "Forming Impressions of Personality," *Journal of Personality,* 23 (1954), 65–76.

waited for the clerk to catch his eye. On his way out, he stopped to chat with a school friend who was just coming into the store. Leaving the store, he walked toward school. On his way out he met the girl to whom he had been introduced the night before. They talked for a short while, and then Jim left for school.

2. After school Jim left the classroom alone. Leaving the school, he started on his long walk home. The street was brilliantly filled with sunshine. Jim walked down the street on the shady side. Coming down the street toward him, he saw the pretty girl whom he had met on the previous evening. Jim crossed the street and entered a candy store. The store was crowded with students, and he noticed a few familiar faces. Jim waited quietly until the counterman caught his eye and then gave his order. Taking a drink, he sat down at a side table. When he had finished the drink he went home.

When the two paragraphs were read separately to different groups of subjects, those who heard the first paragraph pictured Jim as friendly and somewhat extroverted; subjects hearing only the second paragraph viewed Jim as more introverted. To determine the importance of the first impression of a person, the two paragraphs were combined into two patterns: one citing the extrovertive data first and the other citing the introvertive first. Consistently the data presented first had the greater impact on the subjects' perception of Jim. On the trait of "friendliness," for example, 90 percent of the people who heard paragraph one noted Jim to be friendly, as did 71 percent of the subjects hearing the combined paragraph with the extrovertive data first. Only 25 percent of the subjects who heard only paragraph two thought Jim to be friendly; 54 percent of the people who heard that paragraph combined with the introvertive data considered Jim friendly. Thus, with the only variable being the order of the data presentation, the composite impression of Jim differed markedly.[6]

Possibly the first information perceived about a person gives us a "mental set" that we consider more basic than subsequent data.

[6]A. S. Luchins, "Definitiveness of Impression and Primacy-Recency in Communication," *Journal of Social Psychology*, 48 (1958), 275–290.

If in our minds we initially accept Jim as friendly, we may create special circumstances to account for his latter actions. Perhaps he had a bad day at school or is otherwise more bothered. We try to fit the conflicting pieces of data together, by inferring what is going on inside Jim. On the other hand, if we initially react to Jim as unfriendly, we may view his later actions as merely fulfilling some ulterior base motive. Consider how our impression of Jim would greatly affect our response to him and communication with him.

## ENCODING SIMPLIFICATION—STEREOTYPES

As we perceive other people and proceed to encode our impressions, the necessity of classifying the data for memory storage forces us to generalize and simplify. These classifications of people are commonly called "stereotypes." These "pictures in the head" as Walter Lippmann once described stereotypes, permit us to classify quickly and easily, providing ready-made compartments in which to place people.

This phenomenon of stereotyping helps to explain why we may be "unjust" or "biased" in our reactions to social practices, institutions, and other cultures, as well as people. The simplification involved may blind us to the innumerable differences among the members of our self-imposed classification based on such categories as age, race, socioeconomic status, national origin, or sex.

In an experiment designed to note how we tend to react to others in terms of our classification of their status, twenty college students were assigned the task of attempting individually to persuade two people to donate blood to a Red Cross drive. These two people were actually confederates who depicted a sloppily dressed undergraduate and a neatly dressed young instructor. The confederates alternated in the two roles as each persuader came into the room to make his appeal. In every instance both confederates would indicate that they had been persuaded and would donate their blood to the cause. Then the persuaders were interviewed privately and asked such questions as, "Suppose you had to decide that one of the members of the audience said 'yes' because you had forced him to and the other said 'yes' just because he naturally wanted to anyway.

Which would you say you had forced and which one just wanted to anyway?" Nineteen of the twenty persuaders made a distinction, and eighteen indicated that the high-status person (the neatly dressed instructor) had "naturally wanted to follow anyway" while the sloppily dressed undergraduate had been "forced" by the persuasion of the speaker's arguments.[7] A review of this study commented:

> Here, then, were two people responding in the same way to the same persuasive argument, yet the cause of their response was seen quite differently by the persuader. Apparently in our culture to perceive a man as belonging to a high-status group is to perceive his behavior as being internally determined, as showing "free will" and self-determination, whereas to perceive a man as belonging to a low-status group is to perceive him as being easily pushed around by external pressures.[8]

A classic study of stereotyping was conducted at Princeton University in 1932. One hundred students were asked to characterize twelve ethnic groups (including such categories as nationalities and races) from a list of traits. Great agreement was found on such characterizations as:

> Chinese—Superstitious, conservative, sly
> English—Conventional, intelligent, sportsmanlike
> Italian—Artistic, impulsive, passionate
> Japanese—Industrious, intelligent, progressive
> Negroes—Lazy, happy-go-lucky, superstitious[9]

Obviously, our general stereotypes undergo change. The Japanese during World War II were typically viewed as sinister, sly, and warlike, whereas now the prewar stereotype has probably become reestablished. Also consider the dramatic changes in categorical traits imposed by white Americans upon Afro-Americans. No doubt the Black Militants of the sixties have all but erased the Negro stereotype of the thirties.

[7] J. W. Thibaut and H. W. Riecken, "Some Determinants and Consequences of the Perception of Social Causality," Journal of Personality, 24 (1955), 113–133.

[8] D. Krech, R. S. Crutchfield, and E. L. Ballachey, Individual in Society, New York, McGraw-Hill, 1962, p. 54.

[9] D. Katz and K. W. Braly, "Racial Stereotypes of One Hundred College Students," Journal of Abnormal and Social Psychology, 28 (1933), 318–320.

Even with the emancipated role of women within our society, sex still provides a convenient category for making judgments. Women are considered poor drivers, overly emotional, and limited in their capacity for details, particularly mathematical. A 1968 study at the University of Connecticut measured the degree of antifeminine prejudice in women. Forty college girls were given the same writing selection to evaluate, but half of them were told that it was by John T. McKay, while the other half were told it was by Joan T. McKay. John was rated as much more intelligent and persuasive than Joan, even though there was no difference in the material other than the author's name.

The important point to remember concerning stereotyping is that this categorical mode of perceiving people is not a fault found only among prejudiced people. It is done by all of us due to the very nature of our perceptual processes. Our judgment of the competitiveness of a particular Jew, the intelligence of someone with a thick Southern accent, or the honesty of a used car dealer is merely the application to specific individuals of traits associated in our minds with a group. This typically unconscious practice of categorizing is dangerous, however, when it distorts our perception and experience. As we come to know people better their unique personal qualities distinguish them from any group of which they are a part, while broad, hasty judgments based upon our present categories may cause us to misjudge. In the award-winning motion picture, *In the Heat of the Night,* the key interpersonal conflict concerns the perceptions of each other of the white southern sheriff portrayed by Rod Steiger and the black northern detective played by Sidney Poitier. The detective finally breaks some of the sheriff's preconceived opinions of his Negro stereotype, and himself begins to perceive the sheriff as distinct from his category of a stupid "red-neck." Even scholars who carefully guard their objective observations of the world speak of "undergraduates," "black militants," and "the administration" as if some general trait of characteristics was universally applicable. The difference between the scholar and the bigot lies not in the vocabulary or categories utilized, but in the original determination of these generalizations and the care with which they are applied.

The attorney who refuses to accept bearded men on a jury, the school board that refuses to hire unmarried men over thirty, the employer who restricts his applicants to white, Anglo-Saxon Protestants, and the Black who views all policemen as brutal are all engaged in stereotyping, applying categories and predicting about future behavior based upon these categories.

Another means of simplifying our impressions, a general form of stereotyping, is to try to fit people into good-bad, black-white, bipolar dichotomies. It is much easier to dismiss an individual totally for one character trait of which we disapprove than to consider the divergent facets of each individual that we encounter. Thus, all drinkers may be viewed as sinners and the President of the United States is either a "good" or a "bad" President, a judgment often based upon party label.

In many ways our society promotes this two-valued orientation of other people. Our television and movie heroes are typically portrayed as all good, while villains are viewed without redeeming qualities (although we have gained some overt sophistication in dispensing with the white hats on our cowboy heroes and the black hats on the villains). Our two-party political system and our fraternity-sorority-independent splits are facets of such an orientation. When we are in the habit of viewing people as either American or un-American, saved or damned, wholesome or degenerate, we narrow our perceptual capacities by these labels we apply.

There are obviously some categories into which a person either fits or does not—dead or alive, married or single, male or female—but by imposing bipolar frames to other human traits, we ignore the numerous gradations between. To force a person into honest-dishonest, dependable-undependable, clean-dirty, sane-insane, liberal-conservative categories ignores the numerous possible degrees between the two extremes.

Authorities differ on the implications of such two-valued orientations for our mental health. Semanticist Wendell Johnson, for example, believed that a reliance upon a bipolar view of others is the basis for many mental disturbances. He argued that healthy people are more comfortable with numerous classifications for people and their acts while disturbed people are happier when they have to choose between only two possibilities.[10] This belief, however, is chal-

[10]W. Johnson, *People in Quandaries*, New York, Harper & Row, 1946, pp. 294–335.

# 'These Days, Man, You Can't Just Go Around Unpolarized'

lenged by A. R. Luria, who suggests that normal people are more comfortable in using clear dichotomies than are neurotics.[11] Notice how even these critical commentators also rely upon a bipolar division of "normals-neurotics"! For our purposes, however, we should recognize that when we are selectively encoding data about people into only two possibilities, we are possibly distorting our perception of others.

Similar to this dichotomized view of people is a special category of perception behavior known typically as "the halo effect." Acting as a type of filter to our sense perceptions, a strong, favorable view of a person gives us a mental set for judging all his behaviors. As a hypothetical example, consider the behavior of Will Gray, a young history professor and basketball enthusiast. Professor Gray was elated to learn that the university's new basketball star—known for his speed and ball handling—had enrolled in his European history course. Gray took every opportunity to discuss basketball with the young man, and so great was his admiration for his student's basketball talent, he failed to notice that the young man's work was below the standards of most of the other students in the class. When other students complained, Professor Gray attributed their reactions entirely to jealousy.

Conversely, if we have a generally unfavorable impression of a person, we may judge him unusually low on all his personality traits. In both cases we are exaggerating the homogeneity of the personality of an individual. We are guilty of oversimplifying our perceptions.

## OUR SENSORY BASES OF JUDGMENT

While stereotypes are mental categories within us, impressions are formed of people by our sensory reception of cues in the form of facial features, gestures, and voice patterns. These cues provide the basis for our judgments of others.

Many of the inferences we make concerning a person's personality are triggered by visual cues. As suggested in Chapter 1, visual

[11]A. R. Luria, The Nature of Human Conflicts, New York, Liveright, 1932, pp. 292–300.

contact forms the basis for communication on an interpersonal basis. Sociologist G. Simmel has suggested:

> Of the special sense organs, the eye has a uniquely sociological function. The union and interaction of individuals is based upon mutual glances. This is perhaps the most direct and purest reciprocity which exists anywhere.
>
> . . . This mutual glance between persons, in distinction from the simple sight or observation of the other, signifies a wholly new and unique union between them. . . . By the glance which reveals the other, one discloses himself. By the very act in which the observer seeks to know the observed, he surrenders himself to be understood by the observer. The eye cannot take unless at the same time it gives.[12]

Thus, the dynamic nature of the visual interaction is indicated again. We have all traded glances with a stranger across a room. Our desire for communication will depend upon whether we seek or avoid this visual contact.

A part of our impression of another person is based upon his facial features and expressions. Studies confirm that people tend to agree in attributing certain personality traits to faces. This perceptual agreement amounts to a sort of cultural stereotyping. For example, the use of cosmetics and other grooming aids have been demonstrated to affect our judgment of women. The amount of lipstick worn was perceived as related to sexuality, while bowed lips gave the impression of being conceited, demanding, immoral, and receptive to the attentions of men.[13] Hollywood's typecasting and makeup techniques have no doubt influenced the formations of these perceptions.

Another study has demonstrated that, just as personality traits are inferred from facial features, the reverse is also true and facial features are inferred from personality traits. College freshmen at the

---

[12]G. Simmel, "Sociology of the Senses: Visual Interaction," in R. E. Park and E. W. Burgess, eds., Introduction to the Science of Sociology, Chicago, Univ. of Chicago Press, 1921, p. 358.

[13]P. F. Secord, "Facial Features and Inference Processes in Interpersonal Perception," in R. Tagiuri and L. Petrullo, eds., Person Perception and Interpersonal Behavior, Stanford, Calif., Stanford Univ. Press, 1958, pp. 300–318.

University of Nevada were read the following descriptions of two fictitious persons:

1. This man (A) is warmhearted and honest. He has a good sense of humor and is intelligent and unbiased in his opinion. He is responsible and self-confident with an air of refinement.
2. This man (B) is ruthless and brutal. He is extremely hostile, quick-tempered, and overbearing. He is well-known for his boorish and vulgar manner and is a very domineering and unsympathetic person.

The subjects were then asked to consider a list of thirty-two facial characteristics and decide which would likely be found in A and which in B. The students pictured A with neat hair, a direct and upward gaze, widened, bright eyes, a smooth brow, relaxed nostrils, and a smiling mouth; B had slicked down or disheveled hair, an overted, downward gaze, narrowed eyes, a knitted brow, distended nostrils, and a turned-down mouth.[14]

We even feel adept at recognizing emotions from pictures of people. Snapshots, slides, and motion pictures of an actor portraying such emotions as anger, amazement, sadness, religious love, determination, and doubt were shown to observers who could identify the intended emotion some 85 percent of the time.[15] A later study using pictures of people actually reacting to situations involving fear, surprise, humor, etc., found similar results with observers. This study also revealed that certain parts of the face seem to specialize in sending different kinds of signals. We tend to interpret surprise and fear from the upper half of the face. The lower half shows us laughter and happiness. The pleasant emotions were more easily recognized than the unpleasant ones.[16]

In addition to facial expressions other visual cues are given us in a person's gestures and other expressive movements. As discussed in Chapter 1 the unconscious cues that form the basis for our meta-

[14]This study by Linda Johnson is described by P. F. Secord, *ibid.,* pp. 305–308.
[15]D. Dusenburg and F. H. Knower, "Experimental Studies in the Symbolism of Action and Voice—I: A Study of Specificity of Meaning in Facial Expression," *Quarterly Journal of Speech,* 24 (1938), 424–463.
[16]J. C. Coleman, "Facial Expression of Emotion," *Psychological Monographs, 63* (1949), 1–36.

communication are vital components of our person perception. Subtle cues tend to be tied to individual cultures, but certain acts seem to have near universal meaning. The elocutionists of the nineteenth century worked out detailed scientific analyses of the overt expressions of our various feeling and emotions. This mechanistic approach for training public speakers has long been disdained as artificial and unnatural, but the fact remains that visually we are constantly communicating, either reinforcing or distracting from any messages being sent vocally.

Some people are more expressive than others in their visual communication. The highly animated person may appear more open and involved in the act of communicating, but even the stiff, rigid, aloof person cannot conceal himself for long. The person who shrugs his shoulders or waves his hands while speaking without facial emotion may only be reflecting a cultural heritage; yet the receiver of the message will react as if these expressive movements are cues to the personaity. The animated talker is likely to be judged as "forceful" while the immobile speaker is thought to be "controlled" and "cold."

Listeners tend also to judge a speaker's personality by his voice pattern. In one study eighteen male speakers read uniform manuscripts from prepared texts to an audience of six hundred people by means of audio recording. The audience, which did not know the speakers and could not see them, was asked to match certain personality data including photographs and sketches of people to the voices of the speakers. The experimenters concluded that the voice alone conveys some correct information in choosing among age and general personality sketches. Individual personality traits and photographs were matched less accurately. Members of the audience tended to respond in a uniform manner if incorrect in their judgments, and when stereotypes were perceived from the voice (as through accents), all features of the stereotype were attributed to the speaker.[17]

Situations also provide cues for our identification of emotions and forming of impressions, but we do not accord these cues the same status as cues projected by a person's face, movements, and

[17]G. W. Allport and H. Cantril, "Judging Personality from Voice," *Journal of Social Psychology*, 5 (1934), 37–55.

voice. We view the latter as expressions of feelings or emotions and the situation as a determinant of that reaction, as circumstances in which various emotions are more or less probable. This context does give us additional information for the encoding of our impressions.

## ACCURACY OF OUR JUDGMENTS

Receivers of messages vary in their ability to perceive the attitudes, intentions, feelings, needs, and wishes of others. In our interpersonal communication most people make reasonably accurate judgments of one another; yet this slight misjudgment may cause considerable difficulties. The wife may mistake her husband's irritation with himself for a criticism of her, and end up trying to take over the job for him instead of sympathizing with him. The husband may mistake his wife's irritation with the dog for criticism of him, and end up trying to sympathize with her instead of taking the dog off the couch or getting rid of the dog.

As we observe the behavior of others, we are merely inferring with some degree of probability what is going on inside the person. How well we infer depends upon the quality of the cues, how well we know the person, and our capabilities as judges. We have all likely known people about whom we could not tell in certain situations whether they were serious or joking; the cues supplied were inadequate for our purposes.

A college instructor felt ill and abruptly left class early in the middle of a discussion. At the next class meeting the students were asked by the instructor why they thought he had left. Responses included such reactions as: The instructor was angered over the low quality of the discussion and left in disgust; he had an appointment; he thought he had arrived at a good stopping point; he wanted to give the class more preparation time; and he was reacting emotionally to one of the comments made by a member of the class. None of the class guessed the true reason, but all were willing to make inferences concerning the behavior witnessed.

It seems that experience, and the learning that accompanies it, are vital in making accurate judgments of others. Small children become quite adept at "reading" their parents for indications of "how far to go" before actual punishment becomes imminent. Cues of punishment threat are often interpreted with great accuracy. The child, however, is not yet a discriminating observer and may try unsuccessfully to generalize from his parents to all adults. In kindergarten, attempts to cajole the teacher through baby talk and acting "cute" may prove inappropriate responses to threatened discipline.

Intelligence as well as maturity should obviously be related to our skill in judging people. Two kinds of capacity (relevant to our judgment of others) are correlated with intelligence: the abilities to draw inferences about people from observations of their behavior; and to account for observations in terms of general principles, or concepts. A researcher arranged to have some seven hundred pupils in elementary and secondary public schools observe a silent movie. Two scenes of the film depicted a boy engaged in "good" activities while two others reflected "bad" behavior. The children were asked to write their opinions of the boy and what they thought of him. Expert judges then classified these responses as *inferences* if the student attempted to go beyond the action shown on the screen, and *concepts* if the student attempted to explain both the good and the bad behavior by introducing conceptual notions that accounted for the diversity. This analysis revealed that the older the child, the greater the number of inferences and conceptual applications. The girls, on the average, slightly exceeded the boys at all ages in the number of inferences made.[18]

In another study, children rated their father, mother, favorite teacher, best male friend, best female friend, and a younger sibling on a six-point trait scale. The older children varied more in their descriptions. In other words, the older the perceiver, the more differently he rated father, mother, and teacher, for example. Girls perceived the adult figures in a less differentiated and more favorable manner than did males. The investigators suggest that perhaps women, to a greater degree than men, use stereotyping in describing others, and that perhaps this is consistent with the common belief that women react "intuitively" to others and are not able to find

[18]E. S. Gollin, "Organizational Characteristics of Social Judgment: A Developmental Investigation,"*Journal of Personality*, 26 (1958), 139–154.

logical reasons for their personality impressions.[19] Other studies have similarly demonstrated that person perceptions vary systematically with the age and sex of the perceiver.

There is also abundant evidence that, other things being equal, one can judge people with whom he has a common background of experience more accurately than he can judge unknown persons. Members of the same sex or age category, or the same national, ethnic, or religious groups are better judges of one another than would be an outsider. This advantage may result from sharing the same sets of norms, including the meanings attached to special gestures and speech mannerisms, as well as other forms of interpersonal responses. For example, the "straight" social scientist may have difficulty interpreting responses in an interview with groups of students who label themselves "flower children" or representatives of the "New Left." Facetious and satirical responses may be accepted as genuine unless the interviewer becomes adept at recognizing the subtle shades of the metacommunication signals. Similarly, an American who first-names everyone as soon as he meets them will probably be more fully understood by another American who recognizes him as a compatriot and who has similar habits than by an Englishman to whom such habits may be strange. Such familiarity goes beyond mere stereotyped accuracy, the more one knows about any set of phenomena the more sensitive one becomes to small differences within that set. This fact would account for the ability of men and women to understand the behavior of members of their own sex better than members of the opposite sex.

Interpersonal perception establishes the basis for interpersonal communication. With all the variables that affect accuracy to be observed and evaluated, it could scarcely be expected that a person would be equally skillful in judging all people in a variety of situations. However, we are able to ascertain that some people have in fact developed a facility for accurate judgment of others and are able to apply these abilities in a wide variety of situations. Accurate social perception seems to represent a complex set of skills that must be learned. To the extent that we improve our judgments of other people, our ability to communicate with them improves.

[19]A. R. Kohn and F. E. Fiedler, "Age and Sex Differences in the Perception of Persons," *Sociometry*, 24 (1961), 157–164.

## SELF-PERCEPTION

A logical question at this stage would be: "In a chapter dealing with our perception of others, why talk about self-perception?" The answer lies in studies that indicate a high accuracy ability in judging others is partly a function of attributing to others what the judge sees in himself.[20] When the judge and the person perceived happen to be similar, the judge who generalizes to the other what he sees in himself receives a high accuracy rating. This process of projection, commonly called "empathy," not only determines our basis for judgment, but also establishes a link for meaningful interpersonal communication.

As we judge others by reference to ourselves, we likewise perceive ourselves as we observe the reactions of others to us. As mentioned in Chapter 2, at birth we have no innate value system, we cannot observe ourselves directly, and we have no basis for comparing ourselves objectively with other children. We can, however, observe at an early age how other people respond to us, and we learn to tell whether we are worthy persons who merit love and affection or unworthy children who do not. "Shame," "Naughty," and "That's a good boy" become our clues to adult opinion and value judgments about particular actions. We soon conceive of ourselves as objects to be judged.

These reactions of others may mislead a child and cause him to question his worth or adequacy. Many deep personality problems may find their foundations in experiences in which the child develops an unfavorable view of himself. Parents may be responding to their own needs as they mold a child's self-perception without realizing potential dangers.

Social psychologist Roger Brown has pointed out by example that not all of our self-perceptions are merely reactions to particular individuals or family members; even conceptions of geographically remote groups can affect our self-image.

[20] I. E. Bender and A. H. Hastorf; "On Measuring Generalized Empathic Ability (Social Sensibility)," *Journal of Abnormal and Social Psychology*, 48 (1953), 503–506.

*Consider the following rather common transformation in the thinking of a Negro who has grown up in the United States in recent years. We may suppose that, when he was a boy, African Negroes seemed to him to be the painted savages who chased a heroic white Tarzan in Saturday-afternoon movies and American Negroes the forever-inferior descendants of these savages and himself an average American Negro. When he grows older he learns that: 1) The art of African Negroes is as highly regarded by some intelligent people as is the art of Europeans; 2) African colonies can become African nations and produce their own leaders who are treated deferentially by Europeans and American heads of state; 3) American Negroes, the descendants of Africans, sometimes go to college, enter professions, become artists or statesmen. All of this has implications for his self-concept. He comes to think of himself as a young person of some ability and good character who has been given no opportunities. Treatment by whites that once seemed reasonable enough and certainly inevitable now seems a wrong that must be righted. Obstreperous fellow Negroes who used to be considered stupid for inviting trouble now seem to be far-sighted leaders. Acquiescent fellow Negroes who once seemed to be the sensible ones now seem to be the cowardly ones. A change in a man's impression of certain geographically remote others—Africans—might in this way effect a transformation in his impression of himself and those nearest him.[21]*

## SUMMARY

Every minute of our waking day we are reacting to the world around us—the school or office in which we work, the people we work with, our wife or husband, our children, our friends, and all the events of the day. Social perceptions determine our view of ourselves, our reactions to those around us, and our basic orientation to the world. This characteristic mode of responding will be discussed in greater depth in Chapter 4. When interpersonal perception is

[21]R. Brown, *Social Psychology*, New York, Free Press, 1965, pp. 651–652.

viewed as reciprocal on the part of interacting persons, it constitutes an important gateway to other processes of human interaction and in turn helps us to understand a fundamental variable in interpersonal communication.

## Suggested Applications and Learning Experiences

1. Working in pairs, prepare a dialogue between two imaginary students about race relations on the campus. Attempt to determine the attitudes the students have about each other as well as members of other races. How do these attitudes manifest themselves?

2. Using a contemporary film or television drama familiar to all participants, analyze the communication with a view toward interpersonal perceptions. What cues were most indicative of the feelings?

3. Select a picture or cartoon involving people that irritate or disgust you. Share your feelings with members of a group and compare their reactions to it.

4. Why do our perceptions vary? If there are questions concerning hereditary differences in people, research the effects of phenyl-thio-carbamide (commonly called P.T.C.) on the taste of different individuals. How may these differences account for communication problems?

5. Working in groups, prepare a brief questionnaire that you think can categorize members of the class. Some categories may be: What jobs have you held? What are your hobbies? What are your career plans? How serious are you? Compare your evaluations of one another and identify cues that might be misleading from our behavior.

6. In English courses you have likely encountered the term "writer's eye." In public speaking courses the term "audience analysis" is employed. What are the similarities or differences in these terms and the perceptions of members of a communication group?

## Suggested Readings

Berlo, David K., "Observations and Judgments," *The Process of Communication*, New York, Holt, Rinehart and Winston, 1960, pp. 217–235.

Campbell, James H., and Hal W. Hepler, "Persuasion and Interpersonal Relations," *Dimensions in Communication*, Belmont, Calif., Wadsworth, 1965, pp. 87–95.

*Cantril, Hadley, "Perception and Interpersonal Relations," *American Journal of Psychiatry, 114* (1957), 119–127.

Crockett, Walter H., "Cognitive Complexity and Impression Formation," *Progress in Experimental Personality Research*, II, New York, Academic Press, 1965, pp. 47–90.

Gollin, E. S., "Forming Impressions of Personality," *Journal of Personality, 23* (1954), 65–76.

*Haney, William V., "Perception and Communication," *Communication and Organizational Behavior Text and Cases*, Homewood, Ill., Richard D. Irwin, 1967, pp. 51–77.

*Items thus identified are reprinted in Kim Giffin and Bobby R. Patton, *Basic Readings in Interpersonal Communication*, New York, Harper & Row, 1971.

# interpersonal orientations and 4 communication

You are concerned about a close friend. He seems troubled; he smokes more and eats less; he is irritable and not as approachable as usual. Naturally, you wonder if you have done something to antagonize him. Obviously, he needs to be understood. He may be coping with an overwhelming problem, one entirely outside of your relationship with him. Perhaps he is having difficulty with his work or with someone else unknown to you. He may be concerned with an internal conflict such as a sense of frustration that he is not living up to his ambitions or potentialities. Possibly he is unaware that he is showing this difficulty at all because it is beneath his level of awareness. Your ability to "understand" him, that is, to interpret his orientation toward you and your orientation toward him, will determine the effectiveness of your mutual communication.

The focus of this chapter is on a person's habitual orientation toward other people. Closely related to our perception of others is our system of typical responses. In our modern environment most of our actions immediately or ultimately are reactions to other people. We must be able to anticipate, for example, how an instructor views the process of living, what his experiences mean to him, and how he goes about relating to us and to others.

In the business and professional world, understanding others is frequently crucial to one's occupation. An employer evaluating a potential employee is a rather common example. Here what one person is trying to find out about another is primarily in terms of capability, personal goals, potential, and perhaps sincerity. The point is that this orientation toward other people determines our interpersonal relationships and pattern for communication; it involves the study of personality. Intuitively, all of us have become judges of personality based upon our past experiences; an examination, however, of more objectively determined bases for viewing personality could add to our understanding of and effective use of interpersonal communication.

## STUDY OF PERSONALITY AS INTERPERSONAL ORIENTATIONS

The layman views personality as meaning the social qualities of an individual, whether he is exciting, popular, or fun to be with. Our interest in personality is more technical. Personality is here considered to be the basis for what our judgment of a person is, what is significant about him, and how he is likely to act in certain kinds of situations. It includes such items as his intellect, his values, his energy levels, his urges to certain kinds of behavior, and his techniques for getting along with people.

Personality dimensions, that is, significant human behavior patterns, involve both intrapersonal and interpersonal patterns. A representative list of personality characteristics is that developed by Cattell.[1] During the years 1949 to 1957, Cattell and his associates developed techniques for measuring different factors of personality for persons sixteen years of age or older. Originally based upon a comprehensive factor-analysis, Cattell's instrument has been extended to three forms

[1] R. B. Cattell and H. W. Eber, *Handbook for the Sixteen Personality Factor Questionaire*, Champaign, Ill., Institute for Personality and Ability Testing, 1957.

and the factorization analyzed three more times by independent experimentation and a prodigious amount of statistical work.

In addition to the well-known factor of intelligence, Cattell has identified fifteen other factors that comprise the following sixteen characteristics:

| | |
|---|---|
| Aloof vs. Warm-outgoing | Trustful vs. Suspecting |
| Dull vs. Bright (intelligence) | Conventional vs. Eccentric |
| Emotional vs. Mature | Simple vs. Sophisticated |
| Submissive vs. Dominant | Confident vs. Insecure |
| Glum-silent vs. Enthusiastic | Conservative vs. Experimenting |
| Casual vs. Conscientious | Dependent vs. Self-sufficient |
| Timid vs. Adventurous | Lax vs. Controlled |
| Tough vs. Sensitive | Stable vs. Tense |

Each factor should be viewed as behavior which can be identified on a continuum; for example, the last one would be viewed as *behavior* which is somewhere between very stable and very tense. Although this list has items which may appear to overlap, the research completed by Cattell indicates that large numbers of people view each of these factors as distinct or discrete. In addition, each of them is identifiable and measurable.

Many of Cattell's factors are interpersonal in nature, even though they do not appear so at first glance. For example, in the case of the Submissive vs. Dominant continuum, it is impossible to be very submissive when all by yourself; there must be some other person present to whom you can submit. In addition, even those characteristics which are primarily intrapersonal, such as a tendency toward anxiety, clearly imply certain types of interpersonal orientations which will influence interaction behavior. More and more the study of personality is becoming the study of interpersonal behavior patterns, and thus of direct concern to the student of interpersonal communication.

Our purpose here is to review systematic approaches to the analysis of interpersonal orientations, that is, ways in which individuals usually are oriented toward other people as they attempt to communicate with them. There are several systematic approaches. Each is slightly different, indicating that this field of study is in process of being explored, and has not as yet become well stabilized; each systematic approach, however, provides some additional insight into possible improvement of one's interpersonal communication habits.

## SYSTEMATIC APPROACHES TO INTERPERSONAL ORIENTATIONS

A simple conceptual system consists of classifying people as cooperative or noncooperative as to their interpersonal relations. This approach is based primarily on the thesis that most people are motivated to interact with others by the desire to obtain something from them. The basic premise is that people need people; an individual's intrapersonal needs can be satisfied only through others. The person by himself is incomplete—inadequate. He stimulates others through interpersonal communication to provide his needs, whatever they may be—emotional support, acceptance, a sense of adequacy, a sense of power—or reassurance that he will not be harmed, punished, or ostracized. Such a person views others, then, in terms of their potentialities for meeting these needs. We might ask: is this a rather negative view of people? Yes, it certainly is. Is it a justifiable view? On the basis of clinical experience and the amount of research that has been done, it appears that the premise is probably true. Most intelligent, mature people engage in interpersonal trades; that is, they work out arrangements with others whereby they give something needed by other people, for example material or moral support, and in turn receive something needed, such as recognition or status.

Various researchers notably Homans, Thibaut, and Kelley, have surveyed related evidence and developed theoretical models of interaction as "social exchange."[2] These models are based upon the premise that the cost of interaction to the individual, that is, cost in terms of giving something to another person, is balanced against the potential reward in terms of satisfaction of a personal need. In this fashion interactional exchange takes place.

Morton Deutsch has been primarily interested in studying cooperative behavior under conditions which appeared to require in-

[2] J. W. Thibaut and H. H. Kelley, *The Social Psychology of Groups*, New York, Wiley, 1959, and G. Homans, *Social Behavior: Its Elementary Forms*, New York, Harcourt, Brace & World, 1961.

From *The Unexpurgated Memoirs of Bernard Mergendeiler*, by Jules Feiffer. Copyright © 1959, 1961, 1962, 1963, 1964, 1965 by Jules Feiffer. Reprinted by permission of Random House, Inc.

terpersonal trust.[3] Trust is defined by Giffin as reliance upon an object, the occurrence of an event, or the behavior of a person in order to achieve a desired objective, the achievement of which is uncertain in a risky situation.[4]

Deutsch developed two major hypotheses:

1. As there is an increase in an individual's confidence that his trust will be reciprocated, the probability of his engaging in cooperative behavior will increase; and
2. As the ratio of anticipated positive consequences over negative consequences increases, the probability of his engaging in cooperative behavior will increase.

Other hypotheses developed by Deutsch were concerned with the factors that affect the individual's confidence that his trust will be fulfilled; the factors identified were intentions, power, communication, presence of a third person, and the individual's self-esteem.

In his experiments Deutsch utilized a two-person non-zero-sum game in which the gains or losses incurred by each person are a function of the choices made by the two persons. This game is a variation of the prisoner's dilemma which has been described as follows:

> Two suspects are taken into custody and separated. The district attorney . . . points out to each that he has two alternatives: to confess to the crime the police are sure they have done or not to confess. If they both do not confess then the district attorney states that he will book them on some trumped-up charge . . . ; if they both confess, they will be prosecuted, but he will recommend less than the most severe sentence; but if one confesses and the other does not, then the confessor will receive lenient treatment for turning state's evidence, whereas the latter will get the "book" slapped at him.[5]

[3]M. A. Deutsch, "Trust and Suspicion," *Journal of Conflict Resolution*, 2 (1958), 265–279.

[4]K. Giffin, "Interpersonal Trust in Small Group Communication," *Quarterly Journal of Speech*, 53 (1967), 224–234.

[5]R. D. Luce and H. Raiffa, *Games and Decisions: Introduction and Critical Survey*, New York, Wiley, 1957, p. 95.

As an illustration, below, in the design used by Deutsch, person 1 has to choose between rows X and Y, and person 2 has to choose between columns A and B:

|  | | Possible choices of person #2 | |
|---|---|---|---|
|  | | A | B |
| Possible | X | (+$ 9, +$ 9) | (−$10, +$10) |
| choices of | | | |
| person #1 | Y | (+$10, −$10) | (−$ 9, −$ 9) |

Person 1's payoffs are the first numbers in the parentheses and person 2's are the second. The amount of money won or lost by each on any specified trial is thus determined by the *combination* of the choices made by each of the two persons. For example, if person 1 chooses row Y (in an attempt to win $10) and person 2 chooses column B (in a similar attempt to win $10), they each lose $9. Examination of the possibilities of choice for person 1 shows that he can win most and lose least by choosing Y, as person 2 can do by choosing B. But if person 1 chooses Y and person 2 chooses B they both lose. *Both can win only with the AX arrangement.*

Deutsch's subjects were college students who understood the game. Throughout his various published accounts of the use of this game Deutsch has emphasized the principle that: "The essential psychological feature of the game is that there is no possibility for 'rational' behavior in it unless the conditions for mutual trust exist."[6] He went on to generalize that there are many social situations that do not permit rational behavior unless the conditions for mutual trust exist—for example, buyer-seller transactions, husband-wife relations, pedestrian-driver interactions, and a crowd in a theater when there is a fire.

Deutsch's beginning has been significant and beneficial in that he has maintained a very high degree of scientific rigor. From his work and that of his students the following inferences can be drawn concerning interpersonal cooperation.

[6]M. Deutsch, *op. cit.*, p. 270.

1. A cooperative (or noncooperative) orientation on the part of the individual will influence his tendency toward actual cooperative behavior.[7]
2. Communication between the speaker and listener will tend to increase the likelihood of cooperation between them, especially if they express their intentions and expectations of each other and indicate their plan of reacting to violations of their expectations.[8]
3. Increased social power over another person increases the likelihood of the powerful person cooperating with the person over whom he has power.[9]
4. A person will tend to cooperate with another person if he knows they both dislike a specified third person.[10]
5. Cooperative persons tend to have personalities which can be characterized as below average in authoritative or dogmatic orientations.[11]

It must be admitted that this approach to interpersonal orientations is based upon an individual's motivation to further his own personal goals. This orientation assumes a view of human nature that is primarily self-centered, but at the same time exhibits a willingness to cooperate with others under selected conditions. It is entirely possible that genuine, self-dependent altruism does exist; that some people offer help to others out of pure compassion, giving to others without thinking of possible reward in return. No studies, however, have yet emphasized this view of interpersonal orientations.

Instead of viewing interpersonal orientations as a dichotomy of cooperative-uncooperative behavior, another dichotomy has been developed by Milton Rokeach in terms of an "open" or "closed"

[7]M. Deutsch, "The Effect of Motivational Orientation upon Trust and Suspicion," *Human Relations, 13* (1960), 123–139.

[8]J. Loomis, "Communication, the Development of Trust, and Cooperative Behavior," *Human Relations, 12* (1959), 305–315.

[9]L. Solomon, "The Influence of Some Types of Power Relationships and Game Strategies upon the Development of Interpersonal Trust," *Journal of Abnormal and Social Psychology, 61* (1960), 223–230.

[10]J. N. Farr, "The Effects of a Disliked Third Person upon the Development of Mutual Trust," paper presented to the American Psychological Association Annual Conference, New York, 1957.

[11]M. Deutsch, "Trust, Trustworthiness, and the F Scale," *Journal of Abnormal and Social Psychology, 61* (1960), 138–140.

mind.[12] This approach identifies the characteristic way in which an individual receives and processes messages from others. The general degree to which a person will change his attitude toward an object or concept after hearing another person's orientation toward that object or concept is the basis of a scale of open-to-closed-mindedness. Extreme "closed-mindedness" is identified as dogmatism. A dogmatic person is described as follows:

1. Likely to evaluate messages on the basis of irrelevant inner drives or arbitrary reinforcements from external authority, rather than on the basis of considerations of logic;
2. Primarily seeks information from sources within his own belief system—for example, "the more closed-minded a Baptist, the more likely it is that he will know what he knows about Catholicism or Judaism through Baptist sources";
3. Less likely to differentiate among various messages which come from belief systems other than his own—for example, an "extremely radical rightist may perceive all nonrightists as communist sympathizers";
4. Less likely to distinguish between information and the source of the information and will likely evaluate the message in terms of his perceptions of the belief system of the other person.

Essentially the "closed" person is one who rigidly maintains a system of beliefs, who sees a wide discrepancy between his belief system and those belief systems which are different from his, and who evaluates messages in terms of the "goodness of fit" with his own belief system.

It should be readily apparent that the "openness" or "closed-mindedness" of an individual is an index to his interpersonal orientation. In like manner it is an indicator of the way he will interpret your attempts to communicate with him. At this point you as a communicator may attempt to profit in two ways: (1) check your own interpersonal behavior to see if you are sufficiently open-minded to evaluate objectively and use appropriately information which is somewhat incongruent with your prior experience or belief system; (2) become more clearly aware of the degree of open- and closed-

[12]M. Rokeach, *The Open and Closed Mind*, New York, Basic Books, 1960, pp. 61–64.

mindedness of your fellow students and teachers as you attempt to relate and work with them in interpersonal situations.

A slightly more elaborate classification of interpersonal styles has been developed by Karen Horney.[13] Horney was among the leading psychiatrists in asserting that neurotic difficulties must be seen as disturbances in interpersonal relationships. In her theoretical work, she classified people into three types according to their predominant interpersonal response traits: (1) moving *toward* others; (2) moving *against* others; and (3) moving *away from* others.

According to Horney's system *going toward* others ranges from mild attraction to affiliation, trust, and love. Such a person shows a marked need for affection and approval and a special need for a partner, that is, a friend, lover, husband or wife who is to fulfill all expectations of life and to take responsibility for good and evil. This person "needs to be liked, wanted, desired, loved; to feel accepted, welcome, approved of, appreciated; to be needed, to be of importance to others, especially to one particular person; to be helped, protected, taken care of, guided."[14]

Behavior identified as *going against* others ranges from mild antagonism to hostility, anger, and hate. Such a person perceives that the world is an arena where, in the Darwinian sense, only the fittest survive, and the strong overcome the weak. Such behavior is typified by a callous pursuit of self interest. The person with this interpersonal orientation needs to excel, to achieve success, prestige, or recognition in any form. According to Horney, such a person has "a strong need to exploit others, to outsmart them, to make them of use to himself." Any situation or relationship is viewed from the standpoint of "what can I get out of it?"[15]

Behavior which is characterized as *going away from* others ranges from mild alienation to suspicion, withdrawal, and fear. With this orientation the underlying principle is that one never becomes so attached to anybody or anything that he or it becomes indispensable. There is a pronounced need for privacy. When such a person goes to a hotel, he rarely removes the "Do Not Disturb" sign from outside his door. Self-sufficiency and privacy both serve his outstand-

[13]K. Horney, *Our Inner Conflicts*, New York, Norton, 1945.
[14]*Ibid.*, pp. 50–51.
[15]*Ibid.*, p. 65.

ing need, the need for utter independence. His independence and detachment have a negative orientation, aimed at *not* being influenced, coerced, tried, or obligated. To such a person, according to Horney, "to conform with accepted rules of behavior or to additional sets of values is repellant. . . . He will conform outwardly in order to avoid friction, but in his own mind he stubbornly rejects all conventional rules and standards."[16]

Horney summarizes the three types as follows:

> *Where the compliant type looks at his fellow men with a silent question, "Will he like me?"—and the aggressive type wants to know, "how strong an adversary is he?" or "can he be useful to me?"—the detached person's concern is "will he interfere with me? Will he want to influence me or (will he) leave me alone?"*[17]

Horney's classification is a very elementary but still quite useful start on the analysis of interpersonal orientations. As a student of interpersonal communication you may reassess your own interpersonal orientation patterns; you may also learn to identify and deal with different types of interpersonal orientations on the part of your colleagues as you interact and work with them.

A more elaborate and systematic approach to the study of interpersonal orientations has been developed by Schutz in his book, *Fundamental Interpersonal Relations Orientation* (FIRO).[18] Schutz advances the idea that every person orients himself in characteristic ways toward other people, and that knowledge of these orientations allows for considerable understanding of individuals and their interpersonal communication behavior.

The major premise of this theory is that people need people—and each person, from childhood on, develops a fundamental interpersonal relations orientation. Schutz posited three fundamental dimensions of interpersonal behavior—*inclusion, control,* and *affection.* His analysis of the results of a large number of research studies—parental, clinical, small group—shows convergence in their discovery

---

[16]*Ibid.,* p. 78.
[17]*Ibid.,* pp. 80–81.
[18]W. C. Schutz, *FIRO A Three-Dimensional Theory of Interpersonal Behavior,* New York, Holt, Rinehart and Winston, 1958.

of the importance of these three areas, and demonstrates how a measure of these three variables can be used both to test a wide variety of hypotheses about interpersonal relations and to understand and predict interpersonal communication behavior.

Each of these three areas can be divided into two parts—the behavioral characteristics which the individual actively *expresses* toward others, and the degree to which he *wishes* such behavior to be directed toward him.

*Inclusion* concerns the entrance into associations with others. The need for inclusion involves being interested in other people to a sufficient degree that others are satisfactorily interested in oneself. Behavior aimed at gaining inclusion is seen as an attempt to attract the attention and interest of others.

The need to *control* includes the ability to respect the competence of others and the need to be respected by others. It is the need to feel adequate and reliable. Control behavior implies decision-making, and is identified by such terms as "authority," "influence," "dominance," "submission," and "leadership."

*Affection,* unlike inclusion and control, occurs primarily between two people (at a time). It includes the need to love and to be loved. Degrees of affectionate behavior are implied in the terms "friendliness," "caring," "liking," "hate," "loving," and "emotional involvement."

In order to have satisfactory interpersonal relationships, according to Schutz, in each of these three areas *the individual must establish a balance between the amount of behavior he actively expresses and the amount he desires to receive from others.*

As Schutz worked on the development of these three areas he was reminded of the fable of the blind men who disagreed over the characteristics of an elephant (that is, an individual's "need" areas), but apparently each was describing the same elephant. He observed that clinicians discuss "unconscious forces," small group investigators describe "overt behavior," child psychologists report on "early interpersonal relationships," and sociologists are interested in "roles and group structures." It seemed to him that there was decided convergence toward the same set of variables even though the approaches were somewhat different. The problem then, as he saw it, was to give a complete description of the "elephant," that is, a description of the

FIGURE 3. SCHUTZ'S "ELEPHANT."

| | | INCLUSION | | | CONTROL | | | AFFECTION | | |
|---|---|---|---|---|---|---|---|---|---|---|
| | | Self to Other (Actions) | Other to Self (Reactions) | Self to Self | Self to Other (Actions) | Other to Self (Reactions) | Self to Self | Self to Other (Actions) | Other to Self (Reactions) | Self to Self |
| DESIRED INTERPERSONAL RELATIONS (NEEDS) | Act | Satisfactory relation re interaction and inclusion behavior [1] | | Feeling that I am significant | Satisfactory relation re power and control behavior [19] | | Feeling that I am responsible | Satisfactory relation re love and affection behavior [37] | | Feeling that I am lovable |
| | Feel | | Satisfactory relation re feelings of mutual interest [2] | | | Satisfactory relation re feelings of mutual respect [20] | | | Satisfactory relation re feelings of mutual affection [38] | |
| IDEAL INTERPERSONAL RELATIONS | Act | Social [3] | People include me [4] | | Democrat [21] | People respect me [22] | | Personal [39] | People are friendly to me [40] | |
| | Feel | I am interested in people [5] | People are interested in me [6] | | I respect people [23] | People respect me [24] | | I like people [41] | People like me [42] | |
| ANXIOUS INTERPERSONAL RELATIONS (ANXIETIES) | Too much activity — Act | Over-social [7] | Social-compliant [8] | I am insignificant (I don't know who I am; I am nobody) [15] | Autocrat [25] | Rebel [26] | I am incompetent (I am stupid, irresponsible) [33] | Over-personal [43] | Personal compliant [44] | I am unlovable (I am no good, rotten bastard) [51] |
| | Too much activity — Feel | I am not *really* interested in people [9] | People aren't *really* interested in me [10] | | I don't trust people [27] | People don't trust me [28] | | *Really* I don't like people [45] | People don't *really* like me [46] | |
| | Too little activity — Act | Under-social [11] | Counter-social [12] | [16] | Abdicrat [29] | Submissive [30] | [34] | Under-personal [47] | Counter-personal [48] | [52] |
| | Too little activity — Feel | I am not interested in people [13] | People are not interested in me [14] | | I don't *really* respect people [31] | People don't *really* respect me [32] | | I don't like people [49] | People don't like me [50] | |
| PATHOLOGICAL INTERPERSONAL RELATIONS | Too Much | Psychotic (Schizophrenia) [17] | | | Obsessive-compulsive [35] | | | Neurotic [53] | | |
| | Too Little | [18] | | | Psychopath [36] | | | Neurotic [54] | | |

FIGURE 3    SCHUTZ'S "ELEPHANT." Reprinted by permission of the author and publisher from William C. Schutz. *The Interpersonal Underworld.* Reprint Edition. Palo Alto, California: Science and Behavior Books, 1966.

three basic interpersonal need areas, and the ways in which they appear in personality structure, in overt behavior, and in pathological behavior. As he worked on this matrix of interpersonal data he came to call it the elephant (see Figure 3). His goal was to provide a complete description of interpersonal variables, sufficient to provide a framework for integration and future investigation in the field. His "elephant" can be better understood if you realize that its development considered four parameters.

1. *Observability*—the degree to which an action of an individual is observable by others; this parameter is dichotomized into *action* and *feeling*. An action usually is more observable to outsiders; a feeling is usually more observable to the self.
2. *Directionality*—the direction of the interaction with respect to originator and the target of the interaction; this parameter is trichotomized into (a) self toward others, (b) others toward self and (c) self toward self. The first two categories are pretty much self-evident; the last category may be viewed as interpersonal in the sense that it represents interaction between oneself and other persons who have been internalized early in life.
3. *Status of action*—whether the behavior is in the inclusion, control, or affection areas of interpersonal behavior.
4. *State of the relationship*—whether the relation is desired, ideal, anxious, or pathological.

With the development of what he called the elephant, Schutz thus attempted to relate all interpersonal behavior, placing into categories indicative of desired behavior, ideal behavior, anxious behavior (behavior which tended toward interpersonal difficulty) and, lastly, behavior which was clearly pathological and would in almost every case provide an interpersonal relationship which is unhealthy.

Schutz's analysis of interpersonal behavior starts with an analysis of an individual's needs or motivations regarding other people. It should be clear that we cannot deal effectively with our problems of interpersonal relationships unless we take into account our interpersonal communication needs, motivations, intentions, and desires.

In day-to-day interpersonal communication we find it necessary to analyze the behavior of others in similar terms; occasionally we run into evidences of a person's anxieties and tendencies toward difficulty, and on rare occasions we observe evidences of pathological tendencies. Only by properly assessing the motivation and intentions of others can we achieve optimum interpersonal relationships.

Perhaps the most elaborate system for an analysis of interpersonal orientations has been developed by Timothy Leary. In 1949 the Kaiser Foundation initiated a series of investigations with the aim of evolving a systematic theory of interpersonal motivation and a methodology for measuring certain factors in interpersonal communication. In 1955 Leary reported the results of a large research project on the systematic study of overt interpersonal behavior. Leary's system considered in depth the factors of interpersonal motivation. The interpersonal motive of any behavior is determined, according to Leary, by asking: "What is one person doing to the other person? What kind of relationship is he attempting to establish through this particular behavior? What is being communicated?" A father, for example, may employ one or a thousand words to refuse his child's request. The mode, style, and content of two different rejecting expressions may be very different, but their message may be the same—rejection.[19]

In his study of interpersonal motives underlying interpersonal communication Leary developed the following hypothesis: a large percentage of interpersonal communication behaviors simply involve a reflex—an automatic response. Such behaviors are so automatic that they are often unconscious and often even at variance with the individual's own perception of them. Thus, Leary's system is tied to a theory of personality. In identifying the various modes of interpersonal behavior it was not his purpose to analyze the structure or task of a group, but rather the motivation of an individual whose communication behavior primarily produces a certain kind of interpersonal "reflex" or functional, purposive, face-to-face response. These reflexes appear to be automatic, involuntary responses to interpersonal situations, often independent of the content of verbal communication which occurs. They are viewed as spontaneous, purposive methods of reacting to other people. The exact manner in which such responses are expressed may be very complex. They are expressed par-

---

[19]T. Leary, "The Theory and Measurement Methodology of Interpersonal Communication," *Psychiatry, 18* (1955), 147–161.

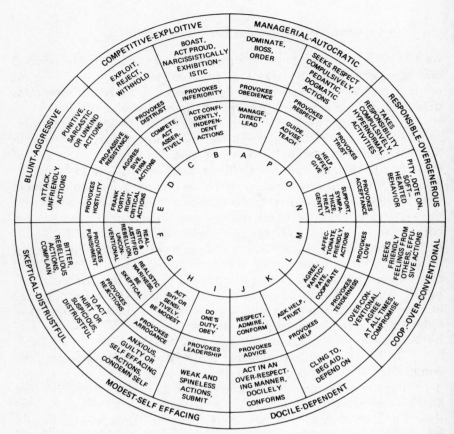

*Classification of interpersonal behavior into 16 mechanisms or reflexes. Each of the 16 interpersonal variables is illustrated by sample behaviors. The inner circle names adaptive reflexes, such as manage. Proceeding outward, the next ring indicates the type of behavior that this interpersonal reflex tends to "pull" from the other one; thus the person who uses the reflex A tends to call up in others obedience. These findings involve two-way interpersonal phenomena—what the subject does and what the other does in return—and are therefore less reliable than the other interpersonal categories presented in the inner and outer rings. The next circle illustrates extreme or rigid reflexes, such as dominates. The perimeter of the circle is divided into eight general categories employed in interpersonal diagnosis. Each of these general categories has a moderate (adaptive) and an extreme (pathological) intensity, such as managerial-autocratic.*

FIGURE 4  LEARY'S CLASSIFICATION OF INTERPERSONAL BEHAVIOR. From Fig. 1. Classification of Interpersonal Behavior into 6 Mechanisms or Reflexes. Timothy Leary, "The Theory and Measurement Methodology of Interpersonal Communication," *Psychiatry* (1955) 18: 147–161; see p. 152. Copyright © 1955 by the William Alanson White Psychiatric Foundation, Inc. and reprinted by the Foundation's special permission.

tially in the content or verbal behavior of the communication and partially in the metacommunication.

The specific details of such human expression require further study; however, Leary demonstrated that the overall, total effect can be reliably rated by observers. His raters, whether trained or untrained, showed impressive reliability in rating what individuals do to each other in their interpersonal situations. The sixteen different interpersonal reflexes are identified in Figure 4. It is important to note that they are called *reflexes,* not simply interpersonal orientations. Leary believed that the reflex manner in which human beings react to others and train others to respond to them in selective ways is the most important single aspect of personality. During any one day, the average adult runs into a wide range of interpersonal stimuli. Thus, the person whose entire range of interpersonal reflexes is functioning well can be expected to use approximately all of the sixteen interpersonal reflexes many times in any one day. There are, however, some persons who show a very limited repertory of only two or three reflexes and reciprocally receive an increasingly narrow set of responses from other persons. Your analysis of your own communication response patterns can lead possibly to improvement through adoption of a wider range of response potential.

Almost everyone manifests certain role patterns which he automatically assumes in the presence of certain other significant persons in his life. These roles probably represent tendencies to express certain interpersonal purposes with significantly high frequency. One of the main implications of this approach is the principle of self-determination, as an individual tends to recreate his interpersonal world along routinized channels. This assigns to the individual the causative responsibility for the interpersonal relations which he works out with others. Leary found that interpersonal reflexes operate with involuntary routine and amazing power and speed. Persons who tend to create interpersonal difficulties appear to be incredibly skillful in drawing rejection, hostility, and similar negative reactions from the people with whom they deal. In many cases such a person is likely to abandon all interpersonal techniques except one which he then handles with magnificent finesse.

A second implication of this approach is the principle of reciprocal interpersonal relations, introduced in Chapter 1. A person's re-

MEN DON'T UNDERSTAND ME. THEY THINK I **TALK** TOO MUCH.

MEN DON'T UNDERSTAND THEY SHOULDN'T LISTEN TO WHAT I SAY- THEY SHOULD LISTEN TO WHAT I **MEAN!**

WHAT I SAY IS BLA BLA BLA- WHAT I MEAN IS BEAUTY AND POETRY.

WHAT I SAY IS GIBBLE GABBLE GIBBLE- WHAT I MEAN IS I AM A LOST SOUL. STUDY MY HAUNTED EYES.

WHAT I SAY IS
HA HA HA HA —
WHAT I MEAN
IS LIFE IS A
WASTE AND
NOBODY CARES
A **FIG** FOR ME.

SOMEDAY I'LL MEET A
MAN WHO WILL IGNORE
MY STUPID WORDS AND
KNOW INSTANTLY THE
FRAGILE, DELICATE,
PERFECTION THAT
LIES BEHIND THEM.

HE WILL SEE
THROUGH ME.
AND OURS
WILL BE A
BEAUTIFUL
LOVE —

I'LL
HURT
HIM.

flex behavior toward another person tends to initiate or invite reciprocal interpersonal responses from that other person; this relationship
then leads to a repetition of the original reflex behavior. In this fashion a person tends to train another person to respond to him in such
a way that the first person continues to produce the kind of behavior
he used in the first place. This reciprocality sets up a cycle which two
people find difficult to break. When the thousands of interactions that
make up each day are studied, this principle becomes increasingly
useful. In Figure 4 Leary has indicated the way in which the initial
response of a person to another in a given context tends to produce
a certain kind of behavior from this second person. It is interesting
to note that Leary, like Schutz, found it desirable not only to identify
certain *kinds* of interpersonal behavior but to show *gradations* ranging
from the normal or well-adjusted individual's behavior to that of the
pathological. Leary's findings should be viewed primarily as theoretical
and developmental. Much more work needs to be done. However,
his systematic approach provides a basis for self-evaluation of one's
own communication response patterns as well as possible ways in
which two or more people can deliberately work toward the improvement of their relationship by giving special attention to their interpersonal communication habits.

## EFFECT OF INTERPERSONAL
## ORIENTATIONS UPON COMMUNICATION

From our survey of systematic approaches to interpersonal
orientations we can identify at least three rather important considerations for the student of interpersonal communication.

In the first place we can infer that *others respond to us within
a framework of the role we indicate that they should play in our interpersonal relationship.* They then can make a choice to play that
role or not to respond to us in the way that we intend. For example,
if we show a desire to control another person, as defined by Schutz,
he will respond according to his willingness to be controlled or refuse to respond to our messages. Of course, he may initiate new
communication concerning the role we have identified for him to play.

In the second place we can infer that *interactions over time tend to train both us and another person to respond to each other in certain ways;* this implication is quite clear from the work reported by Leary. About three years ago an incident occurred which we have talked and thought about many times since: a professor who is one of our colleagues and who is generally well respected was new to our community. After he had been rather well accepted by a number of the staff members, we had an opportunity to meet his wife. His wife was an attractive middle-aged lady. What astonished us was the way in which this professor browbeat her in our presence. He was rude to her, made snide remarks about her, and criticized her behavior, all in the presence of other faculty persons and their wives. We thought his behavior was deplorable and beneath the dignity of a person of his profession. Moreover, we thought that her acceptance of it was a distinct tragedy. We blamed him and pitied her until we read once again the report of the research by Leary. Then it suddenly occurred to us that here was an incident which depicted beautifully the way in which the response of a person to another had produced in turn its own response, which again in turn produced more of the same initial kind of behavior. What had happened was that the two of them had *trained* each other, one to act in a derogatory manner and the other to accept it and to live with it. Now the question occurred to us, which one of them had trained the other, and suddenly we perceived that both of them had to accept equal responsibility. This to us was a new view of a relationship which we originally had thought was the product of the interpersonal communication behavior of only one person. Actually, it was the mutual product of the behaviors of both.

In the third place we may infer that *the misperception of our orientation toward another person can produce confused communication.* For example, we may think our orientation is one of empathy, warmth, and understanding. If our metacommunication or nonverbal behavior is *perceived* by that other person as cool, aloof, and uninterested in him, he will be confused by hearing us say such things as "I see what you mean. . . ." We may wonder why he does not understand what we are trying to say. He will wonder why we bother to say it. Persistent communication confusion of this order can train others to respond to us as one who is generally confused, strange, and difficult to understand.

## SUMMARY

By way of concluding this chapter we should indicate that the development of a science of interpersonal orientations has only begun. The way in which one's interpersonal orientation influences one's own behavior as well as the behavior of others is a fascinating area; it should attract intelligent scholarship for a number of years to come. At this time there is sufficient theory and supporting evidence to indicate that interpersonal communication is highly influenced by the interpersonal orientations of the persons involved, that interpersonal response "sets" or habits may produce desired or undesired responses from others, and that lack of awareness of one's own interpersonal response habits may produce confusion and even hostility as we attempt to establish better relationships with those persons who are near and important to us.

### Suggested Applications and Learning Experiences

1. With one of your classmates play the two-person non-zero-sum (Prisoner's Dilemma) game used in the Deutsch experiments and described above. Play for matches and then play for pennies; note ways in which your own thinking (if any) differs as you raise the value of the "stakes." Note the degree to which it seems to be important for you to "beat" the other person; compare this with your motivation to cooperate in order that both you and the other person may win from the "bank." (Note: for a two-person non-zero-sum game you and the other player will need to contribute initially to a "bank" which can pay off if both of you "cooperate" and both "win.")

2. With two of your friends or classmates hold a brief discussion presenting views on either religion or politics. After each has aired his views and received some responses from each of the other two persons, discuss the degree of open-mindedness each of you has shown. Listen carefully to feedback about your own behavior; reflect on its possible validity. With these same persons hold another discussion on "The Value of This Exercise," once again following it with

a discussion of the open-mindedness of each of you. Note any differences in perceived behavior as the nature of the topic differs.

3. Meet with two of your classmates and ask one of them to act as a nonparticipating observer of the other two as they discuss the value of Leary's "wheel" (Figure 4, Leary's Classification of Interpersonal Behavior). After two of you have discussed this topic to your satisfaction, ask your observer to classify your behavior (as best he can) according to Leary's system. Note very carefully if he has perceived you attempting to "train" the other participant to respond to you in certain ways. Take your turn as observer as two other classmates hold a similar discussion, perhaps on a different topic.

4. With a small group of your friends or classmates (no more than five persons) discuss the following "case" situation. After you have reached a group decision (or spent most of an hour trying to reach a decision) have each member of your group rate each other member on the Interpersonal Perception Scales shown below. As each person receives this interpersonal perception data from other members, data about him becomes his own private property, to be shared with others only if he so desires. Reflect on the possible validity of the data you have thus received. If you have enough courage, ask the others to recall specific instances of your behavior which warranted or did not warrant ratings your received.

## The Nat Bronson Case

Nat Bronson was caught stealing a car from a shopping center parking lot. Nat is fourteen years old. The car was less than a year old and was valued at about $4,000. Nat was seen taking the car, the police were notified, and Nat was caught less than three miles from the shopping center. The car was not damaged. Nat confessed at the time he was caught and again later; there is no question that he is guilty of the theft.

### BACKGROUND FACTS

*Family:*

Nat's mother died when he was born. He was raised by his father, who is known to drink heavily and has a record of many arrests and two convictions, both for armed robbery. At this time the father is being released from prison on parole after serving three and one-half years on a five-year sentence.

Nat has an older brother and sister. He has been living in the legal custody of his older brother, Louis, who is married but has no children. This older brother has been in the Army for two years and is now being sent overseas.

Nat's sister, Sylvia, is married and childless. She and her husband are both eager to have Nat live with them. Nat has often spent weekends in their home, and gone to movies, baseball games, and auto races with them. They like him and are financially able to provide for him. Sylvia's husband, Mike, has a good job, but has been arrested and convicted of gambling, with sentence suspended. Nat says he likes and admires Mike.

*School:*

Teachers say Nat is a poor student but gives them little trouble. He is not well liked by other students; he is quiet and keeps to himself. He is frequently absent and gives minor illnesses as an excuse. He is awkward and uneasy when asked to participate or recite in class.

*Police Record:*

Nat has previously been arrested for stealing automobile tires; however, he was not convicted because of insufficient evidence.

*Nat's Explanation of His Offense:*

Nat could give no specific reason for wanting to steal the car. His comments may be summarized thus: "I felt lonely and miserable. I saw the car owner leave his car without taking the keys. I decided to 'borrow' the car for a little while. I had no real purpose in mind— just drive around for a while. The car was not damaged and nothing in it was disturbed. I would have brought it back."

### Your Task

Your task, as a group, is to come to a decision on what should be done about Nat Bronson. The facts given above may be used in arriving at your decision. Some possible alternatives are the following: (1) place Nat in the state reformatory for four years; (2) place Nat on probation with a second offense leading automatically to the reformatory; (3) place Nat in the legal custody of Mike and Sylvia; (4) place Nat in the legal custody of his father and his father's parole officer; (5) leave Nat in the legal custody of his brother, and his wife, and dismiss the charge of auto theft. Please arrive at a group decision by problem-solving discussion procedures.

## Interpersonal Perception Scale

The questions listed below refer to the group-interaction experience in which you have just participated. The other members of the group will be interested in knowing the ways in which you have perceived them and you will be interested in knowing how they have perceived you. Answer the questions as carefully and honestly as possible.

Read the questions and answer them for each member of the group. Answer each item for each person according to this scale:

| / | 1 | / | 2 | / | 3 | / | 4 | / | 5 | / |
|---|---|---|---|---|---|---|---|---|---|---|
| | Very Little | | Little | | Average | | Much | | Very Much | |

Questions:

1. To what extent does this person *indicate willingness to let others interact with him?* Circle your response: 1, 2, 3, 4, 5.

2. To what extent does this person *show a need to interact with others?* Circle your response: 1, 2, 3, 4, 5.

3. To what extent does this person *express a need to control others?* Circle your response: 1, 2, 3, 4, 5.

4. To what extent does this person *indicate willingness to be controlled by others?* Circle your response: 1, 2, 3, 4, 5.

5. To what extent does this person *express affection toward others?* Circle your response: 1, 2, 3, 4, 5.

6. To what extent does this person *indicate a desire to be shown affection by others?* Circle your response: 1, 2, 3, 4, 5.

## Suggested Readings

*Berne, Eric, "Games," *Games People Play,* New York, Grove Press, 1964, pp. 48–65.

Deutsch, Morton, A., "Trust and Suspicion," *Journal of Conflict Resolution,* 2 (1958), 265–279.

Giffin, Kim, "Interpersonal Trust in Small Group Communication," *Quarterly Journal of Speech, 53* (1967), 224–234.

*Laing, Ronald David, H. Phillipson, and A. R. Lee, *Interpersonal Perception, A Theory and a Method of Research,* New York, Springer, 1966, pp. 23–34.

Leary, Timothy, "The Theory and Measurement Methodology of Interpersonal Communication," *Psychiatry, 18* (1955), 147–161.

*Palmer, Stuart, "Verbalizers," *Understanding Other People,* Greenwich, Conn., Fawcett, 1960, pp. 133–143.

Rokeach, Milton, *The Open and Closed Mind,* New York, Basic Books, 1960, pp. 31–70.

*Schutz, William C., "The Postulate of Interpersonal Needs," *The Interpersonal Underworld,* Palo Alto, Calif., Science and Behavior Books, 1966, pp. 13–33.

*Items thus identified are reprinted in Kim Giffin and Bobby R. Patton, *Basic Readings in Interpersonal Communication,* New York, Harper & Row, 1971.

# the individual encodes and decodes linguistic messages | 5

A plumber wrote the U.S. Bureau of Standards about using hydrochloric acid to clean drain pipes. . . .

Several days later he received this reply, "The efficacy of hydrochloric acid is indisputable, but the corrosive residue is incompatible with metallic permanence."

Confused, he wrote again and asked if the acid "is okay to use or not."

A second letter advised him, "We cannot assume responsibility for the production of toxic and noxious residue, and suggest that you use an alternative procedure."

Still baffled, he wrote, "Do you mean it's okay to use hydrochloric acid?"

A final letter resolved the question.

"Don't use hydrochloric acid. It eats the hell out of pipes."

Symbolization seems to be one of man's primary activities and, as this exchange demonstrates, one not always handled effectively.

Language has often been cited as man's greatest achievement and the major element that distinguishes him from other animals. We have examined the reasons *why* men attempt to communicate, the interpersonal perceptions and the basic orientations toward others that affect their communication. When man attempts to elicit a response he adjusts his symbols to his respondents. We shall now focus attention upon language, our primary means of interpersonal communication.

The first fragmentary utterances of a small child who is just learning to speak indicate the interpersonal nature of human speech. Swiss psychologist Jean Piaget has distinguished two functions of speech for the child: the social and the egocentric. In *social* speech, "the child addresses his hearer, considers his point of view, tries to influence him or actually exchange ideas with him." In *egocentric* speech, "the child does not bother to know to whom he is speaking, nor whether he is being listened to. He talks either for himself or for the pleasure of associating anyone who happens to be there with the activity of the moment."[1] Other investigations have concluded that the bulk of the child's speech, approximately 90 percent, is social.[2] The work of the Russian psychiatrist Vigotsky suggests that even the monologues labeled by Piaget as "egocentric" are actually directed toward *others*. When Vigotsky placed a child who demonstrated the characteristics of "egocentric" speech (babblings, incomplete sentences) in isolation, in a very noisy room or among deaf-and-dumb children, the child's speech dropped off considerably. Vigotsky concluded that the child believes his speech is being understood by others, and when external conditions make speaking difficult or when feedback is lacking, he stops speaking.[3] As we discussed in Chapter 2, the child does not initially clearly differentiate *his* perception of the world from the world as perceived by others. He seems to believe everyone else perceives and understands the world just as he perceives and understands it; thus, others must understand his highly idiosyncratic language. This tendency, as we should see, is not

---

[1]J. Piaget, *The Language and Thought of the Child,* New York, Harcourt, Brace & World, 1926, p. 26.

[2]G. A. Miller, *Language and Communication,* New York, McGraw-Hill, 1951, pp. 155–156.

[3]L. S. Vigotsky, "Thought and Speech," *Psychiatry,* 2 (1939), 29–54.

completely restricted to the child, and lies at the heart of many communication problems. The most important point, however, is that according to available experimental data, *all speech* is a form of interpersonal behavior.

Speech is the term applied to the form and medium of interpersonal exchanges. Man has determined that an oral codification of symbols is best suited for most attempts to elicit response. Language, then, is the systemized body of agreed-upon symbols. The linguistic message, based upon mutual apprehension of common experiences, facilitates joint social action, makes possible the formation of societies, and permits the bridging of cultures and time. In this chapter, we shall examine the basis of "meaning" in speech communication, the inherent problems in our linguistic messages, and language factors that may impede our attempts at effective interpersonal communication.

## THE SEARCH FOR "MEANING"

If communication is concerned with the process of sending and receiving messages, intrinsic to human communication is the attempt to interchange meanings. The very process in which we arbitrarily make certain sounds or symbols *stand for* other things is societal in essence. We can, *by mutual agreement,* make anything stand for anything. This elementary "meaning of words" aspect of communication is important because arguments or disagreements may arise simply because A uses a word one way, and B receives the word as if it meant something entirely different. This could happen when A says, "I was only a *little* late," and B responds, "You were *not!*"

Vigotsky tells the following story illustrating a simplistic misconception of language:

> A peasant listened to two students of astronomy talking
> about the stars. Finally the peasant said: "I can see that
> with the help of instruments men could measure the distance
> from the earth to the remotest stars and find their position
> and motion. But what puzzles me is: How in the devil
> did you find out the names of the stars?"[4]

4*Ibid.,* p. 36.

By permission of Johnny Hart and Field Enterprises, Inc.

Semanticists have, for purposes of clarity, used the analogy of a *map* and the *territory* it represents to describe the relationship between our verbal symbols and the reality for which they stand. The basic aspect of words and language is parallel to the map-territory analogy. Words are symbols which stand for something. The fact that the meanings of many words are shared by many people allows communication to occur.

Social psychologist Roger Brown has offered a reasonable definition of "meaning" as ". . . the total disposition to make use of or react to a linguistic form." To concentrate upon all the possible components in a word or phrase in a literal or absolute fashion, however, presents an unsurmountable problem, as Brown continues: "A man might give all his productive years to spelling out the . . . meaning of a single utterance and find the task unfinished in the end."⁵

Problems resulting from confusion of meanings attached to words are countless, ranging from the attempt of the U.S. Bureau of Standards to communicate with the plumber to situations with far more serious consequences. In a report by W. J. Coughlin in *Harper's Magazine* in 1953, there is a startling suggestion that the mistranslation of a single word may have caused the bombing of Hiroshima and Nagasaki. The word *mokusatsu* has two meanings in Japanese. One is "to ignore," with intent to affront, and the other is "to ignore" as mere withholding of comment. To a surrender ultimatum from the Allies, a message with the "no comment" meaning was prepared; the translator, however, applied the meaning of "refused to notice" as the message was passed on. The first interpretation could have led to surrender with face, while the second forced the Allies to take the drastic action required to end the conflict. According to Coughlin's report, if the misinterpretation of that one word had not occurred, the atom bombs would never have been dropped and Russia would never have entered the Pacific theater, paving the way for the Korean War.⁶

We should examine in some detail those characteristics of language which can lead us to behavior that is at least foolish and at worst tragic.

---

⁵R. Brown, *Words and Things,* New York, Free Press, 1958, p. 100, 103.
⁶W. J. Coughlin, "The Great MOKUSATSU Mistake: Was This the Deadliest Error of Our Time?" *Harper's Magazine,* March 1953.

By permission of Johnny Hart and Field Enterprises, Inc.

*1. Words have different meanings to different people.*

Generally we think of words as having two kinds of meanings or two kinds of definition. One is the *connotative* or *associative* definition. The other is the *denotative* or *operational* definition. The latter kind of meaning refers to the thing or event, a phenomenon to which the word refers. This denotative definition is what we would point to if asked to define a word without being able to speak or use any other words. Such denotative meanings are reasonably stable; they are common to science ($H_2O$), business (debit), industry (arbitration), and to each profession. They mean about the same to everyone, but problems can develop if agreements are not reached. For example, if someone asked you, "What class are you in?" it would be useless to respond unless you knew whether he was referring to class in school or social standing. Even in as restricted an area as parliamentary procedure, to "table" a motion in the United States means to put it aside, while in England the same phrase means, "Let's bring it up for discussion."

Consider the numerous possible meanings in the following story:

> *Struck by a sign in a plumber's window ("struck"?) reading "Iron Sinks," a wag went inside to inform the merchant that he was fully aware that "iron sinks." The storekeeper, ready to play the game, inquired, "And do you know that time flies, sulphur springs, jam rolls, music stands, Niagara Falls, concrete walks, wood fences, sheep run, holiday trips, rubber tires, the organ stops . . .?" But by then the wag had had enough and fled.*

Such multiple meanings inherent in our English language force us to consider context and metacommunication cues to give us more exact meaning. The educated adult uses in daily conversation only about 2,000 of the more than 600,000 words in the English language. Of these 2,000, the 500 most frequently used words have over 14,000 dictionary definitions. Even the term "meaning," which we have attempted to define, has eighteen groups of meanings in a recent dictionary. Further, our language is constantly changing, adding new words, and modifying definitions as usage changes. Figure 5 shows a dictionary definition ascribed to the word *love.*

**love** (luv), *n., v.,* **loved, lov·ing.** —*n.* **1.** the profoundly tender or passionate affection for a person of the opposite sex. **2.** a feeling of warm personal attachment or deep affection, as for a parent, child, or friend. **3.** sexual passion or desire, or its gratification. **4.** a person toward whom love is felt; beloved person; sweetheart. **5.** (used in direct address as a term of endearment, affection, or the like): *Would you like to see a movie, love?* **6.** a love affair; amour. **7.** (*cap.*) a personification of sexual affection, as Eros or Cupid. **8.** affectionate concern for the well-being of others: *a love of little children; the love of one's neighbor.* **9.** strong predilection or liking for anything: *her love of books.* **10.** the object or thing so liked: *The theater was her great love.* **11.** the benevolent affection of God for His creatures, or the reverent affection due from them to God. **12.** *Chiefly Tennis.* a score of zero; nothing. **13.** a word formerly used in communications to represent the letter L. **14. for love, a.** out of affection or liking; for pleasure. **b.** without compensation; gratuitously: *He took care of the poor for love.* **15. for the love of,** in consideration of; for the sake of: *For the love of mercy, stop that noise.* **16. in love (with),** feeling deep affection or passion for (a person, idea, occupation, etc.); enamored of: *in love with life; in love with one's work.* **17. make love, a.** to embrace and kiss as lovers. **b.** to engage in sexual intercourse. **18. no love lost,** dislike; animosity: *There was no love lost between the two brothers.* [ME; OE *lufu;* c. OFris *luve,* OHG *luba,* Goth *lubō*] —*v.t.* **19.** to have love or affection for: *All her pupils love her.* **20.** to have a profoundly tender or passionate affection for (a person of the opposite sex). **21.** to have a strong liking for; take great pleasure in: *to love music; She loves to go dancing.* **22.** to need or require; benefit greatly from: *Plants love sunlight.* **23.** to make love to; have sexual intercourse with. —*v.i.* **24.** to have love or affection, esp. for one of the opposite sex. [ME *lov(i)en,* OE *lufian;* c. OFris *luvia,* OHG *lubōn* to love, L *lubēre* (later *libēre*) to please; akin to LIEF] —**Syn. 1.** tenderness, fondness, predilection, warmth, passion, adoration. **1, 2.** LOVE, AFFECTION, DEVOTION all mean a deep and enduring emotional regard, usually for another person. LOVE may apply to various kinds of regard: the charity of the Creator, reverent adoration toward God or toward a person, the relation of parent and child, the regard of friends for each other, romantic feelings for one of the opposite sex, etc. AFFECTION is a fondness for persons of either sex, that is enduring and tender, but calm. DEVOTION is an intense love and steadfast, enduring loyalty to a person; it may also imply consecration to a cause. **2.** liking, inclination, regard, friendliness. **19.** like. **20.** adore, adulate, worship. —**Ant. 1, 2.** hatred, dislike. **19, 20.** detest, hate.

FIGURE 5 DEFINITION OF LOVE. From The *Random House Dictionary of the English Language.* Copyright 1969 by Random House, Inc. Reprinted by permission.

These dictionary definitions do not tell the complete story, however. Social psychologist Joost A. M. Meerloo has cited some of the potential meanings which the statement, "I love you," may convey:

*This is no essay·on love and no profound treatise on the variations of feelings of tenderness. I only want to show how much semantic difficulty there is in the expression "I love you"—a statement that can be expressed in so many* varied ways. It may be a stage song, repeated daily without any meaning, or a barely audible murmur, full of surrender. Sometimes it means: I desire you or I want you sexually. It may mean: I hope you love me or I hope that I will be able to love you. Often it means: It may be that a love relationship can develop between us or even I hate you. Often it is a wish for emotional exchange: I want your admiration in exchange for mine or I give my love in exchange for some passion or I want to feel cozy and at home with you or I admire some of your qualities. A declaration of love is mostly a request: I desire you or I want you to gratify me, or I want your protection or I want to be intimate with you or I want to exploit your loveliness.

Sometimes it is the need for security and tenderness, for parental treatment. It may mean: My self-love goes out to you. But it may also express submissiveness: Please take me as I am, or I feel guilty about you, I want, through you, to correct the mistakes I have made in human relations. It may be self-sacrifice and a masochistic wish for dependency. However, it may also be a full affirmation of the other, taking the responsibility for mutual exchange of feelings. It may be a weak feeling of friendliness, it may be the scarcely even whispered expression of ecstasy. "I love you"—wish, desire, submission, conquest; it is never the word itself that tells the real meaning here.[7]

Even greater numbers of problems result from the connotative word or expression than from the denotative. While the denotation gives sharpness and accuracy to a word, its connotations give it power. Our most familiar words are rich with connotations—mother, Vietnam, the President. The connotation may even be so strong that it erases the denotation, and for the individual only the connotation then has significance.

This connotative meaning of a word is the thought, feeling, or ideas that we have about the word, the things we say about the word when asked to define it. The words factory worker denotes a person

[7] J. A. M. Meerloo, Conversation and Communication, New York, International Universities Press, 1952, p. 83.

who earns his living by performing productive tasks in a building where many persons are organized to produce a product at a cost below what other people will pay for it. However, the words connote certain feelings and emotions. To some people, *factory worker* may mean a lazy, irresponsible, and apathetic person hostile to management. To others it may connote an honest, good man who is exploited, unjustly treated, and deprived of any freedom and opportunity to exercise responsibility and judgment. In the course of a lifetime, the denotations of words change but little, while our connotations alter with experience.

To some extent, the individual experiences of each of the approximately 300 million English-speaking people differ from all others. Every second of our lives, we are experiencing something that is not exactly the same experience as any other that we have had before, or that anyone else has had. Each individual has certain personal connotations derived from his experience with objects, persons, or ideas that are the referents of the words he uses. General connotations are those accepted as the typical reaction of a majority of people; thus most people in our society regard "war" with fear and abhorrence. This anticipated reaction with its fear overtones can be used then by some persons to manipulate others by simple reaction to the word.

Virtually all words have both denotative and connotative dimensions. The type and degree of reaction to words will vary from person to person. Meanings reside not in words alone, but in the minds of people using them.

2. *Words vary in the degree of abstraction.*

A second major aspect of words and language is that words, like thought and conceptions, vary in degree of abstraction; words are symbols used to represent a generalized category of things, experiences, or ideas. The symbols vary from indicating a total class ("Foreigners"), to a particular class ("Spaniards"), to a specific member of the class ("Juan Martínez"). S. I. Hayakawa has graphically depicted the principle of abstracting with his story of "Bessie," a cow. If we perceive, in front of us, a living organism, we respond, based upon our previous experiences with other similar animals to label the creature we are seeing a "cow." The cow is at the same time unique (different from all other living creatures in certain respects), and a member of a class ("Cows").

**ABSTRACTION LADDER**
Start reading from the bottom *UP*

8. "wealth"

8. The word "wealth" is at an extremely high level of abstraction, omitting *almost* all reference to the characteristics of Bessie.

7. "asset"

7. When Bessie is referred to as an "asset," still more of her characteristics are left out.

6. "farm assets"

6. When Bessie is included among "farm assets," reference is made only to what she has in common with all other salable items on the farm.

5. "livestock"

5. When Bessie is referred to as "livestock," only those characteristics she has in common with pigs, chickens, goats, etc., are referred to.

4. "cow"

4. The word "cow" stands for the characteristics we have abstracted as common to $cow_1$, $cow_2$, $cow_3$ . . . $cow_n$. Characteristics peculiar to specific cows are left out.

3. "Bessie"

3. The word "Bessie" ($cow_1$) is the name we give to the object of perception of level 2. The name *is not* the object; it merely *stands* for the object and omits reference to many of the characteristics of the object.

2.

2. The cow we perceive is not the word, but the object of experience, that which our nervous system abstracts (selects) from the totality that constitutes the process-cow. Many of the characteristics of the process-cow are left out.

1. The cow known to science ultimately consists of atoms, electrons, etc., according to present-day scientific inference. Characteristics (represented by circles) are infinite at this level and ever-changing. This is the *process level*.

FIGURE 6   THE ABSTRACTION LADDER. From *Language in Thought and Action*, Second Edition, by S. I. Hayakawa, copyright, 1941, 1949, © 1963, 1964, by Harcourt, Brace & World, Inc. and reproduced with their permission. Also reprinted by permission of Allen & Unwin Ltd. (London).

This view of language is demonstrated in Figure 6, "The Abstraction Ladder." As the diagram shows, the object we see is an abstraction of the lowest level. As we ascend the ladder, the verbal categories become more general as "Bessie" is placed into broader categories in which we conceive some similarity.[8]

This characteristic of language permits people to avoid one another in arguments by retreating from one level of abstraction to another. Teachers and politicians are often adept at handling difficult questions by changing the level of abstraction when pushed as to specifics. The more abstract we become, the more we are relying upon "what is in our heads" rather than any sort of denotative reality. Former President Eisenhower utilized a shift in levels of abstraction in responding to a question on a television discussion in 1959:

*PRESIDENT EISENHOWER: . . . I'd like to point out that all of the political moves, all of the educational moves you make, must be supported by trade. We must have a better trade. We must have better trade because it is through trade that all of us are going to achieve better standards. And I know this is one subject that is dear to your heart, and it's one I think we should all think about very thoroughly.*

*MR. MACMILLAN: Well, Mr. President, you, we both believe the same thing, I think that these problems in the world can only be solved by the expanding of the wealth and trade of the world. Of course, we are up against quite a lot of pressures, you are and I am. And it isn't always easy to say, it isn't always too easy to do. Yet I think we've done pretty well. And it's a great satisfaction to us to feel that the enormous increase of trade between Britain and the United States [sic!]. You helped us very much with the heavy engineering. I wish you could do something for us on wool textiles but perhaps you'll be able to do that. . . .*

*PRESIDENT EISENHOWER: Let me tell you this: we are concerned about it. I mean we want to see it just as strong*

[8]S. I. Hayakawa, *Language in Thought and Action*, New York, Harcourt, Brace & World, 1964, pp. 173–180.

as you want to see it. I'd like to point out that supporting
this kind of thing is the necessity for broadening our
contacts in the world, particularly—not only among
ourselves—but particularly with the Iron Curtain countries.
I believe we've got to have better exchange of ideas, of the
products and the conclusions of scientific people; we
have got to have more in books; but above all, the people.
I like to believe that the people, in the long run, are going to
do more to promote peace than our government. Indeed, I
think that people want peace so much that one of these days
governments better get out of their way and let 'em have it. . . .

—Eisenhower–Macmillan television discussion,
"Issues Confronting the West," September 1, 1959

Hayakawa has cited a course in esthetics in a large Mid-western
university "in which an entire semester was devoted to Art and Beauty
and the principles underlying them, and during which the professor,
even when asked by students, persistently declined to name specific
paintings, symphonies, sculptures, or objects of beauty to which his
principles might apply. 'We are interested,' he would say, 'in principle, not in particulars.' "[9] When such people remain more or less
permanently stuck at certain levels of the abstraction level, Wendell
Johnson has labeled such a linguistic phenomenon as "dead-level
abstracting." As an example of a persistent low-level abstracting, he
cites:

Probably all of us know certain people who seem able to
talk on and on without ever drawing any very general
conclusions. For example, there is the back-fence chatter
that is made up of he said and then I said and then she
said and I said and then he said, far into the afternoon,
ending with, "Well, that's just what I told him!" Letters
describing vacation trips frequently illustrate this sort
of language, detailing places seen, times of arrival and
departure, the foods eaten and the prices paid, whether the
beds were hard or soft, etc.[10]

[9]*Ibid.*, p. 189.
[10]W. Johnson, *People in Quandaries*, New York, Harper & Row, 1946, p. 270.

This example contrasts sharply with the persistent, high level of abstraction of the professor cited by Hayakawa. Usually, our speech demonstrates a constant interplay of higher- and lower-level abstraction, as we adapt quickly up and down the abstractive ladder.

High-level abstractions are quite useful when they are related to sense-data experience and demonstrate relationships and order. On the other hand, these abstractions can be dangerous as merely evocative terms standing for anything or nothing. The most highly valued terms in our language (love, beauty, truth, etc.) can either be maps without territories or point to specific experiences and feelings. Stuart Chase has summarized the point as follows:

> When we use words as symbols for the abstraction that we "see," they are an abstraction of an abstraction.
> When we use generalizations like chairs-in-general, or "household furniture," we abstract again. The semantic moral is to be conscious of these abstraction levels, and not to lose sight of the original chair.[11]

*3. Language is, by its very nature, incomplete.*

With millions of people reporting their experiences, the same meager store of accepted symbols are used to report to one another what they have experienced. Each common word/symbol must, therefore, necessarily be used to cover a wide range of "meanings." Obviously, the categorized symbols omit details.

In Chapter 3 we discussed our perceptual tendency to simplify by the use of black-white categories and stereotyping. This characteristic of perception is reflected in our language. We are ill-equipped linguistically to describe gradations of differences, so we describe someone as either lazy or industrious, unable to categorize him in any unique fashion.

To be of any value, language must categorize and omit unique details, but this characteristic forces us to overgeneralize. If we fail to recognize that words are only generalized symbols, we are in danger of making certain invalid assumptions:

1. We may assume that one instance is a universal example: "*Nobody* likes me." "*All* women are. . . ." "This *always* happens to me."

[11]S. Chase, *Power of Words*, New York, Harcourt, Brace & World, 1954, p. 55.

"Nothing ever turns out right."

2. We may assume that our perceptions are complete: "Yes, I already know about that."

3. We may assume that everyone shares our feelings and perceptions: "Why didn't you do it the *right* way?" "Why would anyone eat in that horrible restaurant?"

4. We may assume that people and things don't change: "That's the way she is!"

5. We may assume that characteristics that we attribute to people or things are truly inherent: "That picture is ugly." "He's a selfish person."

6. We may assume that our message is totally clear to someone else. "You know perfectly well what I mean." "You heard me!"

While generalizations are potentially dangerous, they cannot be avoided, since language is a body of generalizations. Absolutely perfect interpersonal communication is impossible to achieve because our language is inherently incomplete. Yet there are degrees of incompleteness, and as communicators we should recognize that we are always functioning at levels of probability of understanding. The incomplete nature of our language makes it easy for us to misunderstand one another.

4. *Language reflects not only the personality of the individual but also the culture of his society.*

We have noted that an individual's language behavior necessarily reflects basic features of his personality and that individual experiences and attitudes contribute to different reactions to words. Language, having developed in the context of a certain culture, reflects of necessity that particular culture. In Chapter 2 we discussed the three general categories of cultural differences in communication —formal customs, informal customs, and technological communication patterns. As a derived system of human solutions to recurring human events, experiences, and conditions, *culture* constitutes a system of social organization which differentiates and integrates human interaction and provides guides to behavior and motives to conform.

Language gives us innumerable insights into a culture. As an example of how language mirrors a culture, a study was made of the figures of speech in the language of the Palaun people of the western

From *Boy, Girl, Boy, Girl*, by Jules Feiffer. Copyright © 1959, 1961 by Jules Feiffer. Reprinted by permission of Random House, Inc.

SO IF THEY GET TREATED
NASTY IN A RESTAURANT
OR FOR INSTANCE GET
SHOVED IN THE STREET
THEY THINK IT'S
BECAUSE WE
DON'T **RESPECT**
THEM.

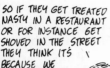

WELL I'VE DISCOV-
ERED AFTER A
LONG LIFE THAT
YOU HAVE TO
**EARN** RESPECT.
IF YOU'RE
NOT IN
**TOO**
MUCH OF
A HURRY-
IF YOU
KNOW
YOUR
PL -

BUT YOU DON'T UNDER-
**STAND!** DON'T YOU SEE
THEY ALL HAVE CHIPS ON
THEIR SHOULDER! SO
NOW IT LOOKS LIKE
IF WE DON'T
SERVE THEM
NICE IN OUR
RESTAURANTS,
THEY'LL
ALL GO
COMMUNIST.

**COMMUNIST!**
AND I USED TO
THINK THEY WERE
ALL SO GOOD-
NATURED. WELL YOU
TURN YOUR
BACK ON
PEOPLE
FOR A
MINUTE
AND—

SO RATHER THAN LET THEM
GO COMMUNIST I SUPPOSE
ITS OUR DUTY TO HELP THEM-
BUT AFTER ALL IT'S A HARD
LIFE FOR **EVERYBODY.** I MY-
SELF DON'T ALWAYS
GET THE BEST SERVICE
IN RESTAURANTS. BUT
**I'M** A GOOD SPORT.
I LAUGH IT OFF.

AFRICA WOULD
BE A LOT
BETTER OFF IF
IT WAS MORE
LIKE YOU, DORIS.

Pacific. Since figures of speech are a means of making the abstract concrete, such an analysis provides unique insights into a culture. To Palauns, a beautiful woman is a "comet." Since maternal descent is more greatly valued than paternal descent, superlative expressions reflect this organizational bias. "Largest" is *"delad a klou"* ("mother of large") and "highest" is *"delad a ngarabub"* ("mother of up").[12]

Even subcultures have language behaviors that distinguish one from another. While we tend to discount class differences in our own society, a team of investigators examined social-class speech differences of people surviving an Arkansas tornado. Ten people were classified as *middle class* by virtue of one or more years of college education and a moderate income. Ten other respondents were matched with them on such factors as age, race, and residence, but who were able to be classified as *lower class* on the basis of income and inadequate education (no schooling beyond elementary school). Analyses of the transcribed tape-recorded interviews revealed the following differences:

a. Almost without exception, descriptions by lower-class participants were given as seen through their own eyes, while middle-class respondents described the acts of others as the *others* saw them.

b. Lower-class respondents demonstrated a relative insensitivity to differences between their perspective and that of the interviewer. For example, surnames were used without identification and pronouns like "we" and "they" had no clear referents. By comparison, the middle-class respondent used contextual clarification of his perspective in an attempt to consider the listener's role.

c. While middle-class respondents used overall frames to organize their entire account, lower-class respondents were basically disorganized, with segmental, limited accounts. Connections between incidents were obscure as respondents tended to wander from one incident to another.

It could be concluded that lower-class respondents perceive in more concrete terms and that their speech reflects these more concrete cognitions. However, as the investigators ask:

> *Does his (the lower-class person) speech accurately reflect customary "concrete" modes of thought and perception,*

[12]R. W. Force and M. Force, "Keys to Cultural Understanding," *Science, 133* (1961), 1202–1206.

*or is it that he . . . is unable to convey his perception? . . .
one concludes that speech does in some sense reflect
thought. The reader is perhaps best left at this point
to draw his own conclusion. . . .*[13]

There is the great temptation to render value judgments on
the language development and behavior of various subgroups, instead
of viewing language differences as merely reflections of cultural ones.
The imposition of linguistic rules formulating language into predictable
sound patterns, a well-ordered grammatical structure and formal
vocabulary facilitates analysis and description of the language, but
does not provide a basis for qualitative judgments. A case of such a
linguistic assumption can be noted in the following citation:

*The syntax of low-income Negro children differs from
standard English in many ways, but it has its own internal
consistency. Unfortunately, the psychologist, not knowing
the rules of Negro non-standard English, has interpreted
these differences not as the result of well-learned rules but
as evidence of "linguistic underdevelopment." He has
been handicapped by his assumption that to develop
language is synonymous with the development of the
psychologist's own form of standard English. Thus he has
concluded that if black children do not speak like white
children they are deficient. One of the most blatant errors
has been a confusion between hypotheses concerning
language and hypotheses concerning cognition. For this
reason, superficial differences in language structures and
language styles have been taken as manifestations of
underlying differences in learning ability. To give one
example, a child in class was asked, in a test of simple
contrasts, "Why do you say they are different?" He could
not answer. Then it was discovered that the use of "do
you say," though grammatically correct, was inappropriate
to his culture. When he was asked instead, "Why are they
different?" he answered without any hesitation at all.*[14]

[13]L. Schatzman and A. L. Strauss, "Social Class and Modes of Communication,"
*American Journal of Sociology, 60* (1955), 329–338.
[14]J. C. Baratz, "The Language of the Ghetto Child," *The Center Magazine, 1* (1969),
32.

Such assumptions evolve because of misconceptions of what language is and how it functions.

Because language thus reflects a particular culture, problems abound when cross-cultural communication is attempted. Although words may mean different things to different people within a cultural grouping, at least some consensus and predictability is possible. The predictability is far less and the potential for misunderstanding is far greater in dealing with nonnative speakers. A young mother from the Middle East, for example, phoned a friend in extreme distress: something must be wrong with her child because her two usual baby-sitters were afraid of the baby. She had called the sitters and both had told her, "I'm sorry, but I'm *afraid* I can't sit with your child tonight."

In addition to the linguistic problems, the cultural differences in values and norms may also lead to communication breakdowns and conflict. The different cultural orientations to time provided the basis for a clash among delegates to the United Nations Educational, Scientific and Cultural Organization in the following illustration:

> One of the most deeply rooted, and largely unconscious, features of any culture is what the psychologists call the time perspective. Within the United Nations, at least three different time perspectives operate.

> "Gentlemen, it is time for lunch, we must adjourn," announces the Anglo-Saxon chairman, in the unabashed belief that having three meals a day at regular hours is the proper way for mankind to exist.

> "But why? We haven't finished what we were doing," replies—in a puzzled manner that grows rapidly more impatient—an Eastern European delegate, in whose country people eat when the inclination moves them and every family follows its own individual timetable.

> "Why, indeed?" placidly inquires the Far Eastern representative, hailing from a country where life and time are conceived as a continuous stream, with no man being indispensable, with no life-process needing to be interrupted for any human being, and where members

*of electoral bodies walk in an out of the room quietly, getting a bite to eat when necessary, talking to a friend when pleasant; but where meetings, theatre performances, and other arranged affairs last without interruption for hours on end, while individuals come and go, are replaced by others, meditate or participate as the occasion requires, without undue strain, stress, or nervous tension.*

*As one or the other group persists in its own conception of the time perspective, as the Anglo-Saxons demand that the duration of meetings and conferences be fixed in advance and that meals be taken regularly at fixed hours, and as the Russians sit irritated and the Latins puzzled and the Secretariat frantic—as this condition continues, mutual friction grows, murmurs of "unreasonableness" are heard around the room; and, when the issue under discussion is an important one, overt accusations are hurled across the room of "insincerity," "lack of serious approach to the program," and even "sabotage."*[15]

If we fail to recognize the diverse ways that the different peoples of the world have attempted to cope with the universal problems of adapting to their environment and the cultural basis for differences between cultures, we lay the groundwork for misunderstanding and conflict.

*5. Language creates a "social reality."*

It is ridiculous to consider language a neutral medium of exchange. Specific words are selected for our use because they do affect behavior. Words call forth internal experiences as if by hypnotic suggestion. The role of language in contributing to man's problems and potential solutions can be shown to contribute to dangerous misconceptions and prejudices.

The color of a man's skin, for example, is tied to plus-or-minus words that inevitably condition our attitudes. The words *black* and *white* in Western culture are heavily loaded—*black* with unfavorable connotations and *white* with positive values. Ossie Davis, Negro actor and author, concluded after a detailed study of dictionaries and

[15]I. Talberg, "They Don't Do It Our Way," *Courier (UNESCO), 3* (1950), 4.

*Roget's Thesaurus* that the English language was his enemy. In the *Thesaurus* he counted 120 synonyms for "blackness," and noted that most of them had unpleasant connotations: *blot, blotch, blight, smut, smudge, sully, soot, becloud, obscure, dingy, murky, threatening, frowning, foreboding, forbidden, sinister, baneful, dismal, evil, wicked, malignant, deadly, secretive, unclear, unwashed, foul, blacklist, black book, black-hearted,* etc., as well as such words as *Negro, nigger,* and *darky.*[16]

In the same book are cited 134 synonyms for the word *white* with such positive connotations as "purity, cleanliness, bright, shining, fair, blonde, stainless, chaste, unblemished, unsullied, innocent, honorable, upright, just, straightforward, genuine, trustworthy, honest," etc. Orientals fare little better than Blacks because "yellow" calls forth such associative words as *coward, conniver, baseness, fear, effeminacy, fast, spiritless, timid, sneak, lily-livered,* etc.

Since these colors are not truly descriptive of races, color designations are more symbolic than descriptive. It seems reasonable and likely that our racial attitudes have been affected by our language. Our culture is not unique in this regard. In the Chinese language, while "yellow" is associated with beauty, openness, flowering, and sunshine, "white" connotes coldness, frigidity, bloodlessness, absence of feeling, and weakness. Similarly, in many African tongues "black" has associations of strength, certainty, and integrity, while "white" is associated with pale, anemic, untrustworthy, and devious. These cultural variables will be discussed later in more detail.

Language provides a basis for grouping aspects of reality together. Linguist Benjamin Lee Whorf studied the ways different languages express simple perceptions: Americans say "I am hungry"; Mexicans say "I have hunger"; Navajo Indians say "Hunger is killing me." He concluded that such differences in expression are connected with differences in cognition. He believed that different cultures perceive the world differently *because* of the restraints imposed by language.[17]

16This study of the effect of language on our prejudices was conducted at Pro Deo University in Rome. It is reported and evaluated by N. Cousins, "The Environment of Language," *Saturday Review*, April 8, 1967, p. 36.
17B. L. Whorf, "Science and Linguistics," in J. B. Carroll, ed., *Language, Thought, and Reality*, New York, Wiley, 1956, pp. 207–219.

Whorf's hypothesis has been argued and contested by psychologists and linguists. The issue is whether language is a mold that determines the shape our thoughts and experiences take or the reverse, that language merely inventories and describes reality. The truth likely resides between the two extreme views. Since, as we have noted, our language is inherently inadequate to reflect all physical reality, a culture emphasizes the differences that are important to it. Thus Eskimos may have many words for snow and Bedouins many words for camel while we have only one. If, however, kinds of snow or classes of camel were important to our lives, we could learn to pay attention to differences. As a child learns a language, he finds ready-made categories into which he can fit his perception. His language, however, not only directs his attention to selected features of his environment but also provides a biased basis for interpretation.

Since language biases our perceptions, we need to be aware of the ways in which words condition our attitudes. If we can understand the basis of our prejudices, we are in a better position to cope with the effects. Hopefully, we can understand the urgency of the slogan that "Black is beautiful."

## THE EFFECT OF WORDS

Implicit in our discussion has been the assumption that words matter; the choice of words in the interpersonal relationship makes a difference to the people involved. If we want a child to move from a particular chair, we ask him to move. If at first our words and vocal emphasis do not impress him, we may try to cajole the child out of the chair, or as a last resort threaten or physically remove him. In our adult world, since most of the action we desire from others cannot be induced by the direct threat of force, we must rely upon speech and metacommunication to achieve any manipulation of others.

Any attempts to manipulate people must be considered on ethical as well as pragmatic grounds. Interpersonal behavior depends to a great extent upon *persuasive* symbol manipulation designed to achieve certain actions from others, based upon some kind of psychological consent. Such efforts might be viewed as unethical when we judge that the action called for will be advantageous to the persuader at the expense of the other person. Language was the instrument of achieving the outcomes in the mixed-motive situations discussed in Chapter 2. The information, if deliberately distorted, can be viewed as constituting unethical behavior.

Skilled salesmen become adept at selecting the key words that appeal to our motives, fears, and desires. Motivational selling has progressed to a fine art with near-scientific procedures. The encyclopedia salesman may induce us to buy because we think we are getting something for nothing, because we want an educated environment for our children, or because his product will make a significant contribution to our lives.

Word association is a common device in eliciting a desired response. A brewer was considering using the word *lagered* to describe his beer and conducted a word association test. Only a third of the people tested gave such responses as "ale," "beer," or "stout." Another third gave such responses as "tired," "drunk," "slow," and "dizzy," while the remaining participants had no response to the word. Thus the word was discarded.

Coined words are often the answer to an advertising campaign problem. Such words as *activated, silicone, Sanforized* and *solium* are products of market researchers who have probed the public mind.

The "social reality" created by words can be used to control the minds of people. For example, a Soviet dictionary is reported to define "religion" as: "A fantastic faith in gods, angels and spirits . . . a faith without any scientific foundations. Religion is being supported and maintained by the reactionary circles. It serves for the subjugation of the working people and for building up the power of the exploiting bourgeois classes. . . . The superstitution of outlived religion has been surmounted by the Communist education of the working class . . . and by its deep knowledge of the scientifically profound teaching of Marx-Leninism."[18]

In a similar vein, Hungarian Reds are reported to have taught their children the following Sovietized version of the Nativity:

> *There was once a poor married couple who had nothing*
> *to eat or dress in. They asked the rich people for help*
> *but the rich people sent them away. Their baby was born*
> *in a stable and covered with rags in a manger.*

[18]*Time*, Jan. 29, 1951, p. 62.

*The day after the baby was born, some shepherds who
had come from Russia brought the baby some gifts.
"We come from a country where poverty and misery are
unknown," said the shepherds. "In Russia the babies grow
in liberty because there is no unemployment or suffering."
Joseph, the unemployed worker, asked the shepherds
how they had found the house. The shepherds
replied that a red star had guided them.*

*Then the poor family took to the road. The shepherds
covered the little baby with furs, and they all set out
for the Soviet paradise.[19]*

The propaganda techniques of Soviet leaders have been studied at the Institute for International Social Research in Princeton,
New Jersey. Hadley Cantril of the Institute believes that an examination of the "official" Soviet language throws light on the "control"
techniques of Soviet leaders because of their explicit assumption
that "an individual's thought and action are guided and molded by
language and words and that, therefore, no inconsistencies or conflicts of meanings can be tolerated." We may note, for example, some
of the "official" definitions cited by Cantril from Soviet dictionaries
and encyclopedias contrasted by standard American translations:

|  | Soviet Meaning | American Meaning |
|---|---|---|
| Individualism | "The-individual-as-a-member-of-a-collec-tive" | "The pursuit of indi-vidual rather than common or collec-tive interests" |
| Freedom | "The recognition of necessity" | "Exemption from necessity, in choice and action; as, the freedom of the will" |
| Charity | "Help granted hypo-critically by repre-sentatives of the dominant class in | "An act or feeling of affection or bene-volence" |

[19]*Newsweek*, Sept. 21, 1953, p. 62.

| | Soviet Meaning | American Meaning |
|---|---|---|
| | societies of exploiters to a certain fraction of the disinherited sectors of the population in order to deceive the workers and to divert their attention from the class struggle" | |
| Initiative | "Independent search for the best way to fulfill a command" | "Self-reliant enterprise; self-initiated activity"[20] |

Are any of us so very different from the Soviet propagandist as we entice, seduce, and coerce (all "loaded" words) others to view the world as we want them to see it? As individual senders of messages, we select the words designed to have the greatest desired effect on the listener. When we want to make a side trip, we tell our fellow traveler (a nonpolitical definition intended) that the trip is "only about a hundred miles," while if we oppose the idea we protest, "Why, that trip is over a hundred miles!" Virtually every utterance that we make reflects a coloring of reality to reflect our feelings, attitudes, and values.

Our language usage creates attitudes and behaviors that would not otherwise occur. The exact words that we use at any particular time reflect our attitudes, feelings, and desires at that time. The same girl may be referred to as: "young woman," "young lady," "miss," "hey-you," "girl," or even "broad" or worse, depending upon the feeling and intent of the speaker.

Columnist Sydney Harris has frequently utilized what he has labeled "Antics with Semantics" to demonstrate how our attitudes determine the words we select.

[20]H. Cantril, *Soviet Leaders and Mastery over Man*, New Brunswick, N. J., Rutgers Univ. Press, 1960, pp. 8, 52, and 58.

*The young nations which oppose our policies
"backward;" the neutral ones are "under-developed"
and the ones supporting us are "developing."*

*I lost the match because I was "off my form;"
you lost because you were "over-confident;" he lost
because he was "too cocky."*

*The academic expert I agree with is a "scholar;" the
academic expert I disagree with is a "pedant."*

*When our statesmen say what they do not really mean,
they are exercising "diplomacy;" when their statesmen say
what they do not really mean, they are engaging in "guile."*[21]

One of the cruelest practices in our labeling process is the remark that tags a person—sometimes for life. Putting a label on a child can influence his entire life—"piggy-fats," "brains," "porky," "gimpy," or "bat" can have either the effect of encouraging the victim to live up to the label or reject the title by changes in behavior. "Clumsy John" may be clumsy all his life unless he is able to forget his label. The label "juvenile delinquent" or "ex-con" may brand a person for life.

The problems of perceptual accuracy discussed in Chapter 3 are thus influenced by our language—our words may filter our perceptions and reflect our evaluation of what we perceive as we communicate with others.

## DECODER PROBLEMS

We spend far more time as receivers of messages than as senders. Just as the sender attempts to elicit a response from the receiver, the receiver must attempt to interpret the genuine meaning in the message. In the interpersonal verbal transaction the receiver fulfills the role of listener.

We have become quite adept at *not* listening. In a society in which we are constantly bombarded with noise we learn to close our

---

[21]S. Harris, "Last Things First," syndicated column appearing in the Chicago *Daily News*, December 18, 1962.

minds to such distractions. Our brain picks and selects those cues having genuine significance. This capacity to shut out and ignore insignificant noise is a genuine blessing but it can lead to listening habits which can adversely affect the capability for interpersonal communication. The listener actually determines whether communication will take place. We can for any reason as receivers shut the speaker off mentally.

Part of the problem can be attributed to the disparity between our thought speed and the rate of a speaker. While we speak in the vicinity of 125–175 words per minute, our thought rate is far greater. We may use this spare time to "detour," to make brief excursions away from the subject, then back to listen. Unlike the reader who loses his chain of concentration and rereads the section missed, however, the listener may have no opportunity for reiteration. The differential between thought speed and speech rate tempts us into the bad habits of daydreaming, shutting out the speaker, and impairing the flow of communication.

Listening, unlike reading, is a socialized activity. Instead of being able to shut out distractions and focus our attention, we are forced to respond to a variety of signals. Whereas we choose the time and place to read, we have no such control over our listening environment. Even after we have received shocking or distressing news, we are still placed in situations when listening is important. A wide variety of emotional and social pressures influence our capacity to listen.

In listening, again unlike reading, the sender controls the message. While we are each able to read at our own individual speeds, we have no such control over the listening process. The speaker may rush and slur over important words that are vital to the message; yet we may have no opportunity to "rerun" the speech in order to correct our listening errors. For social reasons we respond as if we understand completely.

Dr. Ralph G. Nichols, head of the University of Minnesota's Department of Rhetoric and an authority on listening, believes that much bad listening results from an emotional reaction to certain words or ideas that blot out the rest of the message. Consciously watch for the times when you tend to tune out a speaker because you fail to like his personality or his ideas. Even if our goal is to argue him down, we owe it to ourselves to listen fully. Notice the words or thoughts that make you stop listening. Dr. Nichols has found that some of the standard ones are *computerize, fellow traveler, pervert, fink,* and *mother-in-law.* Today some people develop static on hearing words like *mod, cool, beat, hippie, Black Power.* And there are special terms that jar persons involved in certain fields and distort their listening judgment. A man who has been having trouble with a newly purchased house may go "deaf" at the mention of leaks, termites, or contractor; his interest perks up, but he hears mainly his own jangled thoughts. Similarly a person who has been speculating in the stock market may tune out anyone who mentions losses, sharp drop, or sell-off.[22] Thus, we filter incoming stimuli and perceive only those parts of the total pattern which fit our general or specific orientations (biases).

It is also likely that our tendency to evaluate (and thus often reject) as we listen affects our capacity to receive information. The process of reception is impaired if we decide early in the communicative situation that what the other fellow is saying amounts to very little. As renowned psychologist Carl Rogers has stated: "The problem is the very human tendency to evaluate what is said from one's own point of view only, the inability to postpone an evaluation for the sake of communication in the particular situation. This immediate evaluation sets up a chain reaction that colors one's response to a speaker. . . ."[23] Too often we decide to say yes or no before the talker has finished his request or presented all of his reasons and evidence. Often we *appear* to listen to the end, but instead are marshaling our own arguments for use in answering. During this process, naturally, our attention is diverted and we do not listen to what the talker is saying.

An additional problem for the listener is to distinguish between observational statements and statements of *inference.* A speaker may be reporting his perception of reality ("That man lives in a brown house") or drawing inferences from the data ("That man owns his

---

[22]R. G. Nichols and L. A. Stevens, *Are You Listening?* New York, McGraw-Hill, 1957, pp. 90–94.

[23]C. Rogers, "What We Know About Psychotherapy—Objectively and Subjectively," in Wil A. Linkugel et al., eds., *Contemporary American Speeches,* Belmont, Calif., Wadsworth, 1965, p. 40.

home"). Observational and inferential statements are extremely difficult to distinguish because grammar, syntax, and pronunciation offer no clues to the differences. Likewise, the inference may be made with such dynamics and vocal certainty that the "truth" of the statement may go unquestioned. In Chapter 3 we noted the willingness of students to infer motives for the instructor's departure from the classroom ("He had another meeting"), and all were wrong. Inferences are necessary for our behavior and communication, but problems may develop when we tacitly assume statements of inference to be totally factual.

## SUMMARY

In this chapter we have noted some of the reasons why interpersonal communication often fails. The failure may be due to use of words without common referents, variant levels of abstraction, disregard of the connotative power of words, the incomplete nature of our verbal messages, intercultural differences, ignoring other people's points of view, thinking in stereotypes, and the failure to listen accurately. Yet because of the power of language to manipulate and exert control over others, we must exercise judicious care as both encoders and decoders of linguistic messages.

## Suggested Applications and Learning Experiences

1. Meet in groups of five or six students. Each group originates a word which has a justifiable meaning to the group. The members may choose, at random, one member of another group and give him the word to define. He may in turn immediately give the definition or take the option of conferring with other group members. The originating group may challenge his definition. Discuss criteria for judgment.

2. Decide on three isolated, ambiguous words (e.g., *mail, dream, march*). Other members of the class are to make up sentences incorporating the three words. Read the sentences and compare variations in the themes of the sentences, different ways in which specific words are interpreted, etc.

3. Have designated members of your group prepare brief, narrative stories. Send five members of your group out of the room and read a story to someone. As the students return to the room one by one, have the story passed along, and note how the message changes. Ideas may be dropped, added, or modified. Discuss your capabilities as listeners and determine what some of the causes are for bad listening.

4. In groups write up or report a news story in three ways: (1) "straight," objective reporting; (2) slanted positively; (3) slanted negatively. Discuss the objectivity of the news that we read and hear.

5. Collect some "Letters to the Editor" from your school and local newspapers. Observe the language usage and what it tells you about the sender of the message. As groups, generalize your reactions to the techniques employed.

## Suggested Readings

Brown, Charles T., and Charles Van Riper, "Control Speech," *Speech and Man,* Englewood Cliffs, N. J., Prentice-Hall, 1966, pp. 77–97.

Brown, Roger, *Words and Things, An Introduction to Language,* New York, Free Press, 1958, Ch. 5

*Chase, Stuart, " 'Eminent Semantics' and Korzybski's Contribution," *Power of Words,* New York, Harcourt, Brace & World, 1953, pp. 125–150.

*Hayakawa, S. I., "The Language of Social Control," *Language in Thought and Action,* 2d ed., New York, Harcourt, Brace & World, 1964, pp. 101–112.

*Lee, Irving, J., "They Talk Past Each Other," *How to Talk with People,* New York, Harper & Row, 1952, pp. 11–26.

*Items thus identified are reprinted in Kim Giffin and Bobby R. Patton, *Basic Readings in Interpersonal Communication,* New York, Harper & Row, 1971.

# interpersonal contexts and communication | 6

Psychiatrists may note that a patient's behavior is "inappropriate in the situation," while diagnosing a mental disorder. Since situation provides a clue to "nonnormal" behavior, surely we expect the functional communicator to adjust not only to the other people in the communication setting, but to the setting itself. Because interpersonal communication is by definition public or semipublic behavior, certain guides for conduct or social organization may be noted.

We are not concerned with the type of standards imposed by etiquette manuals, but rather those variables in the communication context that ought to make a difference to the participants involved. Understanding the expectations of the situation, the restraints imposed by these factors, and the potential consequences of our acts should assist us in making appropriate communication choices as we interact. Such variables may be classified as either environmental or structural.

## ENVIRONMENTAL VARIABLES WHICH INFLUENCE INTERPERSONAL COMMUNICATION

The physical-social environment has obvious implications for communication expectancies. Let us consider the potential impact on our communication of such variables as: setting or occasion, media employed, and people present.

## Setting or Occasion

If we find ourselves in a particular social situation such as a cocktail party, a picnic, or an evening at the theater, certain patterns of communication behavior are expected. Such occasions usually promote considerable phatic communication designed to demonstrate the "sociable" nature of the communicants. The degree of acquaintanceship determines whether substantive issues are to be discussed.

In his comprehensive work on the social organization of such gatherings, Erving Goffman states:

> Some social occasions, a funeral, for example, have a fairly sharp beginning and end, and fairly strict limits on attendance and tolerated activities. Each class of such occasions possesses a distinctive ethos, a spirit, an emotional structure, that must be properly created, sustained, and laid to rest, the participant finding that he is obliged to become caught up in the occasion, whatever his personal feelings. These occasions, which are commonly programmed in advance, possess an agenda of activity, an allocation of management function, a specification of negative sanctions for improper conduct, and a preestablished unfolding of phases and a highpoint.[1]

We obviously communicate differently with the same people when we change the occasion. The physical space occupied, such as classroom or business office, may determine not only the communicative expectancies, but ultimately the attitudes of the communicants toward one another; the situations for the common presence of people determine the amount, kind, and quality of messages exchanged. In the last chapter we discussed the potential for inference-observation confusion; such confusion is often tied to environmental expectations. For example, a melodramatic international situation developed in 1967 over such a problem. British policemen wrested Vladimir Tkachenko, a young Soviet physicist, from the crew of a Soviet plane

[1] E. Goffman, *Behavior in Public Places,* New York, Free Press, 1963, pp. 4–5.

minutes before its scheduled departure for Moscow. Their explanation was that earlier a witness had heard him shouting for help as he was being forced into a Soviet embassy car.

At that time, the intelligence services of both Russia and the West were particularly alert to spot would-be Soviet defectors. To the Russians, defection was a particularly sensitive subject because of the year's celebration of the fiftieth anniversary of the Bolshevik Revolution and because of the adverse publicity given the most famous defection of all, Joseph Stalin's daughter, Svetlana.

In this case, however, Mr. Tkachenko freely expressed a wish to go back to the Soviet Union after all. He had been quite ill at the time of his departure, and the British inferred that the Soviets had kidnapped him, injected him with a drug, and tried to avoid normal diplomatic procedures by taking the physicist to the airport to smuggle him out of the country. The episode so strained British-Soviet relations that the issue was raised at a meeting of the United Nations.

Our interpersonal communication is unlikely to have so high a degree of intrigue, but nevertheless, the setting or occasion, regardless of its dramatic impact, can greatly influence the ways that our messages are likely to be received.

## Media Employed

The leading spokesman for greater consideration of environmental effects on communication has been Marshall McLuhan. Nearly all the observations that have turned McLuhan into a kind of cult hero have been summed up by Kenneth E. Boulding, Professor of Economics at the University of Michigan. They are:

1. *"A social system is largely structured by the nature of the media in which communications are made, not by the content of these communications."*

2. *"Media can be divided into 'hot' media, which do not involve much participation on the part of the recipient, and 'cool' media, in which the process of communication involves a great deal of participation on the part of the recipient."*

3. *"Print created an 'explosion' resulting in the break-up of an old integrated order . . . Electricity creates an 'implosion' which unifies the nervous systems of all mankind into a single contemporaneous whole, bringing us back to the tribal village, this time on a world scale."*[2]

McLuhan's basic premise seems to be that there have been three Ages of Man—the Preliterate or Tribal, the Gutenberg or Individual, and the present Electric or Retribalized. Each age, he states, is shaped by the form of information available. By information he means not only standard media such as print and television but clothes, clocks, money —anything that conveys meaning. These informational modes or media, he goes on, alter our sensory life. What we see, hear, feel, taste, and smell impel involvement—a big word with him—and thus create a new environment.

From his many relevant observations concerning the influence of environment on our interpersonal communication, one extended quotation from a conversation of McLuhan with G. E. Stern illustrates not only his thesis, but the thesis of this book:

*Communication, in the conventional sense, is difficult under any conditions. People prefer rapport through smoking or drinking together. There is more communication there than there ever is by verbal means. We can share environments, we can share weather, we can share all sorts of cultural factors together but communication takes place only inadequately and is very seldom understood. . . . There is a kind of illusion in the world we live in that communication is something that happens all the time, that it's normal. And when it doesn't happen, this is horrendous. Actually, communication is an exceedingly difficult activity. In the sense of a mere point-to-point correspondence between what is said, done, and thought and felt between people—this is the rarest thing in the world. If there is the slightest tangential area of touch, agreement, and so on among people, that is communication*

[2]K. Boulding, "It's Perhaps Typical of Very Creative Minds That They Hit Very Large Nails Not Quite on the Head," *McLuhan: Hot & Cool*, New York, Signet Books, 1967, pp. 71–75.

*in a big way. The idea of complete identity is unthinkable.
Most people have the idea of communication as something
matching between what is said and what is understood.
In actual fact, communication is making. The person who sees
or heeds or hears is engaged in making a response to a
situation which is mostly of his own fictional invention.
What these critics reveal is that the mystery of communication
is the art of making. What they make in difficulties,
confusions, vague responses is natural. It goes on all the
time in all human affairs as between parents and children,
for example. We are always improvising interpretations
of everything we do, see, feel, and hear. With ingenuity,
with great skill, we improvise responses in order to enable
us to continue our relations with our fellows.[3]*

While much of our attention recently has been directed to
mass media, it would seem reasonable that we extend our concern
to media of person-to-person communication, our words and actions
that elicit responses from others.

**People Present**
In addition to the setting or occasion, and the media variables,
the people present in a communicative setting provide another environmental variable. The mere presence of a second person upon a
scene automatically thrusts a solitary individual into an interpersonal
gathering. Thus placed in social settings, the individual adjusts to expectations of personal appearance designed to elicit responses from
the other person or persons confronted. In Western society, dress
and appearance have been categorized into potential behavioral expectations. We put up a "personal front" that is designed to evoke
certain reactions in public settings. A person may claim that he is
"doing his own thing" through the way he dresses or alters his physical appearance, but he is consciously or unconsciously attempting
to elicit certain types of responses from other people.

A number of research studies have been conducted on the
variable of group size. Researchers have typically found that as size

[3]M. McLuhan, "A Dialogue: Q. & A." *McLuhan: Hot & Cool,* New York, Signet
Books, 1967, pp. 283–284.

of the group increases, the most active participant becomes more and more identifiable as both a communication initiator and receiver, and other, less participative group members become less differentiated in communicative amounts.[4] As size increases, the degree of feedback decreases, producing loss of communication accuracy and increased hostility.[5]

One study examined some correlates of group size in a sample of twenty-four groups ranging in size from two to seven members. These groups met four times to discuss problems centered on human relations. After each meeting members were asked to evaluate group size as it influenced group effectiveness. Members of five-man groups expressed most satisfaction; members of larger groups felt their groups wasted time and that members were disorderly, aggressive, too pushy and competitive; members of groups with less than five members complained that they feared expressing their ideas freely through fear of alienating one another.[6]

These inferences were limited to mental, decision-making tasks. However, other works with "opinion" tasks tend to confirm these results; they also show communication behaviors different for odd-numbered versus even-numbered groups in degree of disagreement and antagonism. An even-numbered opinion split in a small group of two, four, or six members may produce impasse, frustration, and unwarranted hostility. This difficulty was most marked in groups of only two members, a fact of relevance to marriage partners.[7]

How does group size influence productivity in creative groups? One researcher has found that larger groups produced a greater number of ideas, though not in proportion to the number of members. That is, there were diminishing returns from the addition of members. This may be due to the fact that as the size of the group increased, a larger and larger proportion of the group members experienced

[4]R. F. Bales, "The Equilibrium Problem in Small Groups," in T. Parsons, R. F. Bales, and E. A. Shils, eds., *Working Papers in the Theory of Action*, New York Free Press, 1953, pp. 111–161; and P. A. Hare, "Interaction and Consensus in Different Sized Groups," *American Sociological Review*, 17, 261–267.
[5]H. J. Leavitt and R. A. H. Mueller, "Some Effects of Feedback on Communication," *Human Relations*, 4, pp. 401–410.
[6]P. E. Slater, "Contrasting Correlates of Group Size," *Sociometry*, 21 (1958), 129–139.
[7]R. F. Bales and E. Borgatta, "Size of Group as a Factor is the Interaction Profile," in P. A. Hare, E. F. Borgatta, and R. F. Bales, eds., *Small Groups: Studies in Social Interaction*, New York, Knopf, 1955, pp. 396–413.

inhibitions which blocked participation. The researcher also noted that if he deliberately undertook to increase inhibitions to participation by formalizing group procedures, a reduction in the number of ideas contributed was brought about.[8]

The communication setting or occasion, the media employed, and the people present are significant environmental variables that affect our interpersonal communication.

## SOCIAL STRUCTURAL VARIABLES WHICH INFLUENCE INTERPERSONAL COMMUNICATION

When individuals gather to communicate, structural patterns emerge that can be classified and studied. Researchers have long been interested in what happens in group communication. The structural variables which have received most of the attention can be classified as: (1) goal or task orientation, (2) member status, (3) norms, (4) power-structure, (5) cohesiveness, (6) role-functions, (7) member personality, and (8) communicative patterns.

### Goal or Task

Groups, and any other interpersonal relations of any duration, face the continued problems of carrying out the purpose or task of the group and of maintaining good working interpersonal relationships. In Chapter 2 we discussed the reasons why the individual needs to communicate. When a collection of people systematically gathers (and forms a "group"), there is usually some common goal or task to be accomplished. If communication is poor within the group, there is no effective way of working toward the agreed-upon task.

A person will work for a group goal only if he believes that its achievement will satisfy his own wants. Industrial studies of the relationship between worker morale and productivity emphasize the importance for the acceptance of group goal or the *perceived relevancy* of group goals to individual wants. The members must, in other words, see group goals as personally want-satisfying.

The group is constantly challenged by both problems of task

[8]C. A. Gibb, "The Effects of Group Size and Threat Reduction upon Creativity in a Problem-Solving Situation," *American Psychologist*, 6 (1951), 324 (abstract).

completion and membership maintenance. These two levels of concern interactively affect each other. Similarly, levels of work-emotionality should be recognized. The feeling that group members have about the work they are doing obviously has an impact upon their behavior; it is important to realize that there is a large variety of group and individual purposes always present. This variety of individual and group purposes, feelings, and needs, while not openly recognized as the concern or "task" of the group, nevertheless affects the way in which the group accomplishes its task. This level has been labeled by human relations workers as the "hidden agenda." In the midst of this complex of levels, individuals communicate with one another and attempt to achieve a common goal.

## Member Status

This variable refers to the relative position of one of the communicators determined by the degree to which he possesses or embodies some socially approved or generally desired attribute or characteristic. As we may well imagine, these status distinctions are potent factors for group communication.

Investigators indicate that high-status people communicate more than low-status people, that highs communicate more with highs than with lows, and that lows communicate more with highs than with other lows.[9] A research team at New York University in 1958 tested the hypothesis that in biracial work groups the pattern of communication will be similar to the pattern in all-white status hierarchies. Negro and white male college students were employed to work in groups of four—two Negroes and two whites who were total strangers—on a series of tasks that took approximately twelve hours. Interaction classification of the communication showed:

1. The whites made more remarks than the Negroes.
2. The whites spoke more to one another, proportionately, than to the Negroes.
3. The Negroes spoke more to the whites than did the whites to the Negroes.

[9] J. L. Hurwitz, A. F. Zander, and B. Hymovitch, "Some Effects of Power on the Relations among Group Members," in D. Cartwright and A. Zander, Group Dynamics, New York, Harper & Row, 1953, pp. 483–492.

4. The Negroes spoke more to the whites, proportionately than to one another.[10]

These results indicate that the pattern of communication between Negro and white when thrown into contact with one another is reflective of the prevailing status differential of the time. Replication would be needed before such conclusions could be assumed valid today.

There is some evidence that the type of communication presented by low-status people may be very unfriendly when such lows have strong hopes of rising in status. Although these findings are consistent with psychological theory, two major problems have not been solved in research on status—the classification of the bases for status ranking, and determination of the significance of these status dimensions:

1. Status consensus—communicators' agreement on status of other communicators;
2. Status congruency—agreement on an individual's status rankings among other communicators; and
3. Status stability—the tendency for any status rank to persist over time.[11]

Status consensus, congruency, and stability have all seemed to be related to communication, but these relationships are not clear. One study, for example, determined that when people were highly agreed upon the status of a person as a "talker," they also showed high agreement on his status as a "receiver," a provider of "best ideas," and "guidance."[12]

Status achievement has a dual role; in addition to influencing the nature of the interpersonal communication, it also is in turn influenced by communication. An increase in individual prominence is correlated with increased amounts of giving and receiving messages.[13]

[10]I. Katz, J. Goldstein, and L. Benjamin, "Behavior and Productivity in Bi-racial Work Groups," Human Relations, 11 (1958), 123–141.
[11]A. R. Cohen, "Upward Communication in Experimentally Created Hierarchies," Human Relations, 11 (1958), 41–53.
[12]R. F. Bales and P. E. Slater, "Role Differentiation in Small Decision-Making Groups," in R. F. Bales, T. Parsons, et. al., Family, Socialization, and Interaction Process, New York, Free Press, 1955, pp. 259–306.
[13]Ibid.

However, the degree to which a person is liked is inversely correlated with amount of talking. Low-status people use an increase in the amount of communication with high-status people as a means of raising their own status. Studies of emergent leadership tend to support this point. Walter H. Crockett found, for example, that emergent leaders were:

1. Significantly higher than the other people in amount of communication;
2. Significantly higher in amount of communication designed to facilitate discussion; and
3. Contributed information and suggestions significantly more often than did others.[14]

### Norms

If a collection of people can be characterized as a group, certain norms and conformity behavior may be identified. The concept of group norms was derived from long usage in sociopsychological studies. It identifies the ways in which members of a group behave and ways which are thought by them to be proper. Norms may be viewed as a set of directions bestowed by the group to all its members concerning their behavior. Through interaction members find out the group's standards. For example, a young woman elected by her sorority as a representative to the student council may find that such membership is important because it improves her status and provides opportunities for influence. To be an effective member of the student council, she must first determine what is expected of members. This natural "period of adjustment" accounts for the fact that freshmen in the U.S. Senate are seen, but rarely heard.

The relationship between norms and communication has received considerable attention. Members who do not conform initially to group norms are the targets of greater amounts of communication, usually of an instructional nature; if they continue as nonconformists, the tendency is to give them rejecting communication and eventually little or none of any kind. The degree of rejection is a direct function of the cohesiveness of the group and the degree to which the non-

[14]W. H. Crockett, "Emergent Leadership in Small, Decision-Making Groups," *Journal of Abnormal and Social Psychology, 51* (1955), 378–383.

conformist is deviant.[15] These results do not hold for just any collection of people, but for groups where belonging is attractive to its members. In some tightly knit, highly cohesive groups a nonconformist is almost immediately rejected upon detection, in which case communication is both minimal and rejective.

Such conformity to group norms is in actuality a yielding to group pressures, explicit or implicit. Conflict arises when the individual tends to react or to respond in one way, but group pressures force him another. Thus, when an individual has to express his opinion in a group on a particular issue and he knows his personal conviction is at variance with group attitudes, he may either choose to remain independent of group consensus and possibly suffer the consequences, or conform.

The television show Candid Camera used situations employing the principle of group pressure in a number of stunts. A person getting on an elevator in which everyone (confederates) was facing the back would naturally face the back. If everyone in line at a sales counter pats his head while talking with the clerk, the unsuspecting victim can be expected to do likewise.

In Chapter 3 we discussed how group pressures to conform can actually alter our perceptions. The systematic experiments of Solomon Asch have dramatically demonstrated this power of group pressure. In his basic experiments, groups of seven to nine college students were assembled and given the following instructions:

> *This is a task which involves the discrimination of lengths of lines. You see the pair of white cards in front. On the left is a single line; on the right are three lines differing in length. They are numbered 1, 2, and 3 in order. One of the three lines at the right is equal to the standard line at the left—you will decide in each case which is the equal line.*

> *You will state your judgment in terms of the corresponding number. There will be twelve such comparisons. As the number of lines is few and the group small, I shall call upon each of you in turn to announce your judgment, which I shall record here on a prepared form. Please be as accurate*

[15]S. Schachter, "Deviation, Rejection, and Communication," *Journal of Abnormal and Social Psychology*, 46 (1951), 190–207.

*as possible. Suppose we start at the right and
proceed to the left.*

All but one of the students were confederates who were instructed
to give unanimously incorrect responses to items. The one experimental student sat near the end of the row, so that his announced
decision would come after most other members of the group. With
such pressure, 37 percent of the experimental subjects conformed
to the group pressure and were thereby in error.[16] In numerous repli-
cations with a variety of modifications, results have been similar.
Obviously, the other variables discussed above influence the degree
of conformity pressure.

In such a group-pressure situation, the individual naturally experiences cognitive dissonance (discussed in Chapter 2). There may
be dissonance arising from the discrepancy between his judgment
and the group judgment (in which case he may rationalize or suppress
such differences) or between what the individual believes and actually says or does. This "expedient" conforming forces the individual
to project any blame regarding his actions onto others. Mob phenomena such as lynching attests to such involvement.

### Power-Structure

Researchers in the area of group interaction have given considerable attention to the power structure or influence structure within
a group. Measures have been made of the general and specific (to a
situation) influence of members, of opinion-shifts caused by influential members during group discussions, and of behaviors taken as
indicators of influence. Of course, these measures may be tapping
other dimensions, but members of small groups usually can identify
and agree upon a rank order of powerful members in a group.[17]

The most consistently observed relationship between power
of a group member and his communication behavior is a tendency

---

[16]S. E. Asch. "Effects of Group Pressure upon the Modification and Distortion of
Judgments," in H. Guetzkov, ed., *Groups, Leadership, and Men*, Pittsburgh, Car-
negie Press, 1951, pp. 177–190.

[17]A total summarization of the research studies contributing to the conclusions here
cited is found in a monograph by K. Giffin, "The Study of Speech Communication in Small-Group Research." Lawrence, Kansas, Communication Research
Center, Univ. of Kansas, 1968.

toward a greater amount of communication. The direction and content of the communication flow are also influenced by the power structure in a group; orders seldom flow up a power hierarchy, while other types of communication, notably compliments, frequently do. Upward communication may substitute for upward locomotion in a power structure; communication may be used to minimize danger of hostile acts from power superiors and such a power superior may use communication to justify his position to his subordinates.[18]

In a study involving a group of mutually well-known members, communication from influential members was more frequent and intense as the task confronting the group was more relevant to their interests; but in groups of less-familiar members, communication from influential members did not vary with task relevance.[19]

A major factor in the power structure of the group is the pattern and style of leadership, a variable to be discussed under role functions.

### Cohesiveness

Cohesiveness is the primary characteristic of a collection of individuals if they are to be labeled a group; it is the factor which defines its psychological boundaries and differentiates it from other, perhaps larger and less precise, social units. Other dimensions of group behavior, including personality, leadership, and group size are obviously interrelated.

A group with high cohesiveness is one in which the members are highly attracted to the group. Conformity is likely to result due to the interdependence and dedication. In such groups, communication is more equal in amount, more intense, and more valued by members than in groups with low cohesiveness. The "sense of belonging" has been demonstrated to be a significant variable to the success of a group. For example, one study of white-collar workers in a public utility company found that absenteeism increased with decreasing group cohesiveness.[20]

[18]H. H. Kelley, "Communication in Experimentally Created Hierarchies," *Human Relations, 4* (1951), 39–56.
[19]J. G. March, "Influence Measurement in Experimental and Semi-Experimental Groups," *Sociometry, 19* (1956), 260–271.
[20]F. Mann and H. Baumgartel. *Absences and Employee Attitudes in an Electric Power Company,* Ann Arbor, Mich., Survey Research Center, Institute for Social Research, Univ. of Michigan, 1952.

Both the opportunity to talk and to be perceived as a contributing member of the group are contributing factors to group cohesion. Thus, feedback is vital if cohesiveness is to be achieved.

The application of the significance of cohesiveness can be readily observed in team sports or games. Only when an individual is willing to sacrifice "self" for the good of the team effort, will the team likely be successful. A football team may be unaware of the term "cohesiveness," but the concept lies at the heart of the team effort. Similarly, when a teacher is able to transform a class into a cohesive unit, then genuine learning is likely to take place.

## Role-Functions

Roles or role-functions are commonly conceptualized in the literature on small groups as a set of behaviors functionally related to the goals of the group. Research on experimental groups has demonstrated that roles tend to appear in a relatively short time, require different but specifiable sets of behaviors, and have performance criteria set by the group members. Factor analysis of a large number of alleged role-functions has revealed three major factors:

1. *Individual prominence,* i.e., a higher amount of communication given and received;
2. *Aiding group goal attainment,* i.e., presentation of "best ideas" and general suggestions for guidance of group thinking; and
3. *Sociability,* i.e., the characteristics of being well-liked by members and demonstrating emotional stability.[21]

The relationship of the roles to communication is quite clear. The role of "prominent individual" correlates with amount of talking and being talked to by other group members.[22] The amount of verbalization is well correlated with best ideas and guidance; however, individuals who achieve the sociability role, i.e., those who are well-liked, generally do not give or receive as much verbalization and ordinarily do not present the best ideas for guidance of the thinking of the group.

Role-function studies are consistent with the results of the group-member status studies cited earlier in this chapter. There still

---

[21]L. G. Wispe, "A Sociometric Analysis of Conflicting Role-Expectation," *American Journal of Sociology,* 61 (1955), 134–137.
[22]Bales and Slater, *op. cit.*

remains somewhat of a problem of separation of the concepts of status and role. In a study of status-consensus, Slater found high inter-correlation of rank order of roles involving (1) talking, (2) receiving communication, (3) presenting best ideas, and (4) guidance of the group toward its goal. This was particularly true of persons with high status performing these roles. These results seem to point toward the possibility of a role for at least one member of a group as an active "task specialist" who is not particularly well-liked, but quite communicative; and at the same time the possibility of a role for at least one other member of the group as "best-liked" man, emotionally stable, a group pacifier, and much less verbal.[23]

A certain cross-relationship between the variable, role-function, and another variable which we have previously discussed, power-structure, requires explanation. The literature crossing these two variables frequently appears under the label of leadership studies, and utilizes either a functional or a situational approach.

The functional orientation to leadership was developed under the influence of Kurt Lewin,[24] founder of field theory in social science, from subsequent theorizing and research in "group dynamics" and, to some extent, from the human relations movement. With this approach, emphasis is placed on a study of the group rather than the leader as a person. One major aim has been to discover the kind of behaviors that are necessary for a group to survive and attain its goals. In this context, leadership is defined as all those member acts that aid in the development of the group and accomplishment of the group's task. Thus, leadership may be performed by one or many members of the group. It is viewed as a quality that a person may display in varying degrees rather than as something he possesses entirely or not at all. Consequently, leadership may be "possessed" to some degree by any member of a group, regardless of his formally designated office or position.

This functional approach assumes that groups (and leaders) are continually faced with two interrelated tasks:

1. Groups must find ways to deal with problems associated with the

[23]P. E. Slater, "Role Differentiation in Small Groups," American Sociological Review, 20 (1955), 300–310.
[24]K. Lewin, Field Theory in Social Sciences, New York, Harper & Row, 1951.

attainment of agreed-upon goals, i.e., resolve *task problems*; and

2. Group members must find ways to improve and strengthen the group itself, i.e., resolve *maintenance problems*.

Those member (or leader) functions that seem to be effective in moving groups toward resolution of task problems include such acts as asking for clarification of issues at hand, summarizing the contributions of others, proposing new ideas and courses of action, giving and receiving information, and coordinating the ideas and suggestions made by others. Member or leader functions that seem to aid in the resolution of internal problems and maintenance of the group include giving minority views a chance to be heard, mediating and harmonizing conflict within the group, maintaining open channels of communication, and ventilating feelings for the group.

In a study of the leadership patterns of naval officers in forty-six different naval organizations, it was found that the relative emphasis placed upon particular leadership functions was highly influenced by the task situation. While all officers did some coordinating, this function was most frequently stressed in the work of the executive officer. The function of exercising administrative control was most prominent in the activities of the district medical officer; technical supervision was most frequently observed with the electrical officer; and consultation was practiced most often by the legal officer.[25]

It has been argued by such writers as W. A. Whyte that research developing out of the functional approach fosters "group-think" decision-making, and procedures that encourage the leader to give his decision-making functions to subordinates. Whyte asserts that this focus upon groups only encourages conformity, mediocrity; and a loss of individuality in leaders.[26] However, it should be noted that the functional analysis of leadership behavior makes no value judgments as to whether a leader should or should not produce a particular leadership pattern (i.e., democratic, autocratic, laissez-faire). It only asks the question of what consequences are associated with different leadership behavior, and it then leaves to the practitioner the

[25]R. M. Stogdill, "Studies in Naval Leadership, Part II," in Guetzkow (ed.), *op. cit.,* pp. 134–155.
[26]W. A. Whyte, *The Organization Man,* New York, Simon and Schuster, 1956.

problem of deciding what particular leadership practice should be employed in a given situation.

Researchers utilizing the situational approach to study leadership focus upon the situation in which leadership occurs. They operate on the assumption that the traits and skills that characterize a "good" leader will vary from group to group and from situation to situation. Associated with this assumption is the notion of "emergent" leadership, which postulates that temporary or situational leaders will arise in groups when necessary to meet the demands of a new situation. This "new" leader theory has been documented by such researchers as Crockett, who found that when a designated leader failed to provide the leadership functions he was supposed to perform, other members provided them, so there would be a minimal loss in group effectiveness.[27]

Situation-oriented research has assumed that it is unreasonable to expect one leader always to be able to do everything better than anyone else. In a study of street gangs, it was reported that the particular activity of the group was a major factor in determining who would be the gang leader.[28] Similarly, a study of the leadership patterns among college women points to the significance of situational factors. The girls chosen as "intellectual leaders," such as house president, were found to be superior to their peers in judgment, initiative, and intellectual ability. Those girls selected as "social leaders" were generally superior to others in dress and appearance. Finally, girls selected as "religious leaders" were reported as being less "neurotic" than the others. Surprisingly enough, or perhaps not so surprising, the social leaders were found to be the most "neurotic."[29]

While our behavioral scientists are making progress in understanding the phenomena of leadership, the research cannot specify the "proper" practices for all situations.

### Members' Personalities

The personality of a group member obviously can have significant effects upon group behavior, or so it seems. The problem, as we

[27]Crockett, op. cit.
[28]F. M. Thrasher, The Gang, Chicago, Univ. of Chicago Press, 1927.
[29]M. D. Dunkerly, "A Statistical Study of Leadership among College Women," Studies in Psychology and Psychiatry, Washington, D. C., Catholic Univ. of America, Vol. IV, 1940, p. 6.

noted in Chapter 4, is that personality as a variable is difficult to conceive and to measure.

Early leadership studies centered upon "traits" of group leaders in an attempt to isolate those factors such as intelligence and attitude that contributed to effective leadership. When the emphasis changed to leadership *functions*, the transition was also made to member functions and personality variables. The work of Schutz and Cattell cited in Chapter 4 fits this category of research.

In recent times, personality dimensions have been viewed as responses to interpersonal stimuli in identifiable group situations, rather than the common stereotyped approach of self-contained, stabilized personality traits. Berkowitz developed a "response-hierarchy" of behaviors ranked in terms of probability of occurrence in changing situations involving different demands (group expectations of the individual). He determined experimentally that changing situations produced different sets of responses from the individual, including varying degrees of amount, rate, and type of communication with respect to aggressivity-passivity.[30] This work points up the importance of the organization of personality characteristics in terms of probability of interpersonal response behavior.

## Communicative Patterns

By isolating members of a group from one another while they are attempting to accomplish some task, it is possible for the experimenter to control the pattern of communication or form a controlled channel or "communication-net."

One research approach has focused upon observer records; it produces a general picture of the group in terms of volume and type of content of communication. This technique, developed by Robert Bales, has provided the following conclusions:

1. Members do not seem strongly bound by a group decision unless they have participated in making it.
2. An "optimum" balance between number of positive reactions to negative ones is about two to one.
3. A high rate of disagreement and antagonism leads to difficulty in decision-making.
4. There can be too many agreements and too few disagreements.

[30]L. Berkowitz, "Personality and Group Position," *Sociometry, 19* (1956), 210–222.

5. Successful groups seem to follow a sequence of "phases" in problem-solving. These phases are:
   a. problems of orientation
   b. problems of evaluation
   c. problems of control
   d. negative reactions
   e. positive reactions
6. Successful groups seem to have two leaders, one who contributes "best ideas" and another who is "best-liked"—a task leader and a social leader.[31]

These findings suggest possible relationships between types of communication content and such variables as norms, cohesiveness, status, role-function, power-structure, and task achievement.

A quite different approach, employing a systems-research orientation, is that of Alex Bavelas in his study of "communication-nets." Bavelas was clearly interested in the relationships between communication patterns and other variables of group behavior. However, the communication patterns were highly constricted for experimental purposes, being limited to either-or, some-or-none communication opportunities between selected individuals in a group. For example, one type of "net" would allow person A to communicate with person B, and B with C, but A could not communicate with C. Extensions were made of such "chain" patterns, along with the development of "circular patterns" and "wheel patterns" (with one person at the "hub"). The primary concept emerging is that of "centrality." This concept was operationally defined as the *sum* of linkages required of all members to communicate directly and/or indirectly with all other members of the group *divided by the sum of the* linkages needed by one member of the group to communicate with each of the other members. Thus, in an A-B-C-D-E chain, C has the highest centrality.[32]

Research studies have consistently reported that the net structure both directly and indirectly influences group communication and task performance. First, the greater the connectivity of the net, the higher the level of satisfaction in the group. Second, the likelihood of emerging as leader of the group increases with the centrality of one's

[31]R. F. Bales, "In Conference," *Harvard Business Review,* 32 (1954), 44–50.
[32]A. Bavelas, "Communication Patterns in Task-Oriented Groups," *Journal of the Acoustical Society of America,* 22 (1950), 725–730.

position in the net. Third, the individual member's satisfaction with his position in the net is similarly related to its centrality: persons occupying central positions in a network have been found by various investigators to be more satisfied than persons occupying peripheral positions. These results, however, must be viewed as mainly suggestive because of limitations imposed by experimental conditions.

## SUMMARY

In this chapter we have attempted to identify the situational variables that affect our interpersonal communication. Adjustments to our physical-social environments are typically subconscious and unintentional; however, a realization of the import of such factors, usually beyond our control, should help us better understand our communication behaviors.

## Suggested Applications and Learning Experiences

1. Many of your class activities have involved discussion in small groups. Evaluate these discussions, trying to find out why some were more successful than others. Consider both the factors that helped and the factors that hindered discussion.

2. Think of the most successful discussion in which you have participated: Did it have an assigned leader? Was some organizational plan followed? Was everyone in the group active? Was the group able to achieve consensus? Determine some criteria for measuring the success of a group experience.

3. Attend a group meeting outside of class (campus, church, community). Analyze the group in terms of the communication variables suggested in this chapter.

4. Read the book *Thirteen Days, A Memoir of the Cuban Missile Crisis* by Robert F. Kennedy (New York: Signet Books, 1969). Discuss the book with your classmates by considering the environmental and structural restraints imposed by the situation on the communication. How might the decision-making have been improved?

5. Meet in groups and agree upon a problem that you would like to discuss and attempt to arrive at some solution. Research the topic and hold your discussion with observers present who can offer

evaluations and suggestions on your communication. Respond to the criticism with a self-analysis of your capabilities as a communicator in groups.

## Suggested Readings

*Eisenson, Jon, J. Jeffery Auer, and John V. Irwin, "Psychology of Group Discussion," *The Psychology of Communication,* New York, Appleton-Century-Crofts, 1963, pp. 253–269.

*Festinger, Leon, "Informal Social Communication," *American Journal of Psychiatry,* 1957, 119–127.

*Goffman, Erving, "Face Engagements," *Behavior in Public Places,* New York, Free Press, 1963, pp. 83–111.

Hall, Edward T., "Space Speaks," *The Silent Language,* Doubleday, 1959, pp. 146–164.

Martin, Howard H., "Communication Settings," *Speech Communication: Analysis and Readings,* Boston, Allyn and Bacon, 1968, pp. 58–84.

*Items thus identified are reprinted in Kim Giffin and Bobby R. Patton, *Basic Readings in Interpersonal Communication,* New York, Harper & Row, 1971.

# barriers to interpersonal communication | 7

One view of human communication that we have suggested is that successful communication means the overcoming of inherent potential barriers. We have previously discussed some of the environmental conditions that can limit or deter interpersonal communication, such as language and cultural differences.

In this chapter we wish to focus on problems of a more personal nature that frequently limit the effectiveness of human interaction. Four very significant problem areas of interpersonal relations will be discussed in this chapter: (1) interpersonal trust; (2) defensive communication; (3) "gaps" between people; and (4) feelings of alienation. To the extent that these problems can be avoided or resolved, to that extent your interpersonal communication can be greatly enhanced.

## INTERPERSONAL TRUST

The importance of trust in human relations has received considerable attention in the literature of social science, religion, and philosophy. Gordon Allport's theory of personality development through social encounter places trust at the foundation of a satisfying interpersonal relationship.[1] The essays of Erich Fromm on the art of loving[2] and of Martin Buber on the nature of warm human relationships[3] place personal trust at the center of their theories. Such essays are penetrating and exceedingly insightful, and the importance of personal trust in our relations with others is hardly to be questioned. However, thoughtful and penetrating as they are, such essays leave us personally wistful and restless for ways to achieve such relationships with those about us. How can we, who are not blessed with interpersonal genius, achieve a relationship which is full and spontaneous, open and frank? How can we go about achieving the relationship described by Fromm where people care for, show responsibility toward, have respect for, and understand each other?[4] What are the conditions for development of trust?

In an attempt to determine the nature of an effective helpful relationship between psychiatrist and patient, Carl Rogers developed his theory of client-centered therapy; to him, a sense of "psychological safety" was necessary for the patient, and this relationship could be produced by the therapist only if he gave complete acceptance to the patient.[5] Rogers has used the same approach to the problem of helping ordinary people (that is, those who are not mentally ill) to improve their daily relationships with others. If you wish other people to trust you more readily give them acceptance and a sense of non-threatening empathy, warmth, and genuineness.[6]

In a long-range (1953–1964) series of analyses of behavior in human relations training groups ("sensitivity" or T-groups), Jack Gibb has explored the relationship between interpersonal trust and primary dimensions of group behavior.[7] His emphasis on the need for a supportive climate is very similar to Rogers' requirement of a sense of

[1]G. W. Allport, *Personality and Social Encounter*, Boston, Beacon Press, 1960.
[2]E. Fromm, *The Art of Loving*, London, Allen & Unwin, 1962.
[3]M. Buber, *I and Thou*, Edinburgh, T. & T. Clark, 1957.
[4]Fromm, *op. cit.*, p. 25.
[5]C. R. Rogers, *Client-Centered Therapy*, Boston, Houghton Mifflin, 1951.
[6]C. R. Rogers, *On Becoming a Person*, Boston, Houghton Mifflin, 1961.
[7]J. Gibb, "Climate for Trust Formation," in L. P. Bradford, J. Gibb, and K. D. Benne, eds., *T-Group Theory and Laboratory Method: Innovation in Re-education*, New York, Wiley, 1964a, pp. 279–309.

psychological safety. In 1964 Gibb reported that, according to his research, people in groups were inevitably concerned with four basic goals: gaining personal acceptance, exchanging information, achieving a group goal, and controlling each other.[8] He reported that the acceptance goal is primary to the others, that is, it must be obtained before the others can be achieved; and that the achievement of a climate of acceptance hinges upon the development of interpersonal trust. Gibb's work demonstrated that attempts at persuasion in the early life of a group produced distrust, cynicism, and suspicion. On the other hand, communication which was descriptive (not evaluative), problem-oriented (not oriented toward interpersonal control), spontaneous (not strategic), empathic (not insular), equality-oriented (not indicative of superiority), and expressive of provisionally held views (not dogmatic) produced a climate of interpersonal trust.

### Interpersonal Trust: A Construct

Trust is here defined as an attitude in the sense of involving cognitive, cathectic, and conative tendencies.[9] It involves *cognition* of a situation;[10] it involves *cathect* in terms of degrees of positive or negative feelings;[11] and it involves *conation* as a "latent variable," a *potential for action* under certain conditions.[12]

It is important to distinguish the difference between an attitude of trust (the introspective orientation which is a potential for action) and the action itself (trusting behavior). It is common knowledge that one's attitude toward another person may not always be reflected by one's observable actions. Thus, behavior which may *appear* to be based upon an attitude of trust may not always be so.

An example of what may appear to an observer as trusting behavior might be instructional communication to an employee by a job supervisor followed by the implementations of these instructions

[8]J. Gibb, "Defensive Communication," *Journal of Communication, 11* (1964b), 141–148.
[9]H. C. Triandis, "Introduction," in Triandis, et al., *The Behavioral Differential: An Instrument for the Study of the Behavioral Component of Social Attitudes,* unpublished manuscript, 1964, pp. 1–11.
[10]T. M. Newcomb, "An Approach to the Study of Communicative Acts," *Psychological Review, 60* (1953), 393–404.
[11]L. L. Thurstone, "Comment," *American Journal of Sociology, 52* (1946), 39–70.
[12]A. L. Edwards, *Techniques of Attitude Scale Construction,* New York, Appleton-Century-Crofts, 1957, pp. 5–9.

by the employee. Actually, this employee may *not* trust his supervisor at all, but do the job "as instructed" because his own experience warrants it.

It appears to us that in an interpersonal relationship trusting behavior involves these conditions:

1. A person *(P) is relying* upon another person or persons.
2. *P is risking* some potential loss.
3. *P is attempting* to achieve some goal or gain.
4. This desired goal is viewed by *P* as *uncertain.*
5. *P's potential loss* if his trust is violated *is greater than his potential gain* if his trust is fulfilled.

Note that each of the elements listed above is requisite for a trusting situation to occur; however, *it is extremely important to note that, even when all of them are present, there is no guarantee that an attitude of trust is also present.* Information about trust as an attitude must be obtained *in addition* to the observation of the conditions of trusting behavior listed above if you want to know whether or not other people trust you.

Trusting behavior in the communication process can be defined *as reliance upon communication behavior (speaking and/or listening) of another person while attempting to achieve a desired but uncertain objective in a risky situation.*

Recently Giffin produced a theoretical formulation of the trust paradigm in the communication process.[13] This paradigm includes both *inter*personal and *intra*personal trust:

1. *Trust of a speaker* by a listener, called *ethos* by Aristotle and *source credibility* by Hovland, Janis, and Kelley;[14]
2. *Trust of a listener* by a speaker, called *sense of psychological safety* by Rogers,[15] *perceived supportive climate* by Gibb,[16] and *speech anxiety* as described by Giffin and Bradley;[17]

[13]K. Giffin, "Interpersonal Trust in Small Group Communication," *Quarterly Journal of Speech, 53* (1967a), 224–234.
[14]C. Hovland, I. L. Janis and H. H. Kelley, *Communication and Persuasion,* New Haven, Conn, Yale Univ. Press, 1953, p. 21.
[15]C. Rogers, *Client-Centered Therapy, op. cit.,* p. 41.
[16]J. Gibb, "Climate for Trust Formation," *op. cit.,* p. 298.
[17]K. Giffin and K. Bradley, "Group Counseling for Speech Anxiety: An Approach and a Rationale," *Journal of Communication, 19* (1969), 22–29.

3. *Trust of oneself as a speaker*—a person's perception of himself as a communicator who is capable of achieving a desired goal in a situation perceived as "risky" or threatening (the opposite of *speech anxiety);*

4. *Trust of oneself as a listener*—a person's perception of himself as a listener who is capable of achieving a desired goal in a situation perceived as risky or threatening.

In this chapter we shall concern ourselves primarily with the elements of interpersonal trust—trust of speakers and trust of listeners.

## Personal Trust of a Speaker

Trust both influences and is influenced by various elements in the communication process. For example, our trust of a person is influenced by his reliability as we perceive it. On the other hand, the degree of trust we have for this person influences the communication behavior of both of us as well as the results of our interaction. The relationship between these variables is reflexive—as trust increases, certain interaction patterns change; and in turn, their change tends to increase the degree of interpersonal trust.

The manner in which one person's perception of another influences personal trust has been of major concern to many scholars; however, interest has been focused primarily upon the first element of the trust paradigm (described above): *trust of a speaker by a listener* (*ethos* or source credibility). In his *Rhetoric,* Aristotle suggested that *ethos,* the estimation of a speaker by a listener, is based upon the listener's perception of three characteristics of the speaker: (1) intelligence (correctness of opinions), (2) character (honesty), and (3) goodwill (favorable intention regarding the listener).

Hovland and his associates defined source credibility as the resultant value (combined effect) of "(1) . . . the extent to which a communicator is perceived to be a source of valid assertions (his 'expertness') and (2) the degree of confidence in the communicator's intent to communicate the assertions he considers most valid (his 'trustworthiness')."[18] It is clear that these writers attempted to combine the factors of character and goodwill under the single concept of perceived intent to be a reliable communicator.

[18]Hovland, Janis, and Kelley, *op. cit.,* p. 21.

Recently Giffin reported a detailed analysis of studies of interpersonal perceptions as they relate to interpersonal trust.[19] Although
the evidence is not entirely clear, interpersonal trust appears to be
influenced by a listener's perceptions of the following characteristics
of a speaker:

1. *Expertness* relevant to the topic under discussion; this expertise
   may be in the form of quantity of pertinent information, degree
   of ability or skill, or validity of judgment.
2. *Reliability;* this may be perceived as dependability, predictability,
   consistency, or intentions of the trusted person regarding the
   goals or objectives of the person doing the trusting.
3. *Dynamism;* that is, behavior perceived as more active than passive
   and more open or frank than closed or reserved.

Further evidence has been obtained by Giffin which demonstrates
that these three dimensions constitute the attitude space of personal
trust.[20] These three characteristics of a person are perceived directly
by another person, and each may influence interpersonal trust. It
seems quite obvious that, if you wish to have others trust you, you
should adopt behaviors which will demonstrate that you are expert,
reliable, and dynamic. In this way you may hope to overcome this
barrier to interpersonal communication.

As you attempt to demonstrate your expertness, reliability, and
dynamism you will need to be quite open and frank and ready to
relate with other people. Now, some people appear to be quite willing to express themselves openly and frankly to a group of listeners;
other people appear to be hesitant and fearful of doing so. The question can be raised: what kinds of attitudes, thoughts, and feelings inside a person tend to make this difference?

Fear and hesitancy to communicate have been given various
labels: "stage fright," lack of confidence as a speaker, communicator
withdrawal tendencies, and speech anxiety. Clearly the problem is
related to speech if "speech" is used in its broadest sense: to refer

[19]K. Giffin, "The Contribution of Studies of Source Credibility to a Theory of Interpersonal Trust in the Communication Process," *Psychological Bulletin, 68* (1967b),
104–120.
[20]K. Giffin, *An Experimental Evaluation of the Trust Differential: Research Monograph R/19,* Lawrence, Kans., Communication Research Center, Univ. of Kansas,
1968.

to all communication settings, not just public speaking. Also, there is little question that anxiety of a type specific to communication settings is involved. For these reasons we will refer to this phenomenon as "speech anxiety."

The problem of speech anxiety appears to involve a number of personality characteristics, one of which is a person's self-concept. This particular personality characteristic is directly related to the degree of trust a person has for other people.[21]

## The Self-Concept and Trust of Others

Almost without question in our Western culture there is nothing quite so important as one's concept of oneself. This cultural trait places severe emphasis on one's ability to protect his self-image. It is common knowledge that many times people have given up material wealth, personal health, and even their lives to preserve a self-image.

One's cognition of oneself is obtained, in part, by personal sensory perception, and also, in part, by checking with other people. As we discussed in Chapter 2, social psychologists in the tradition of Cooley and Mead hold that a person's impressions of his mind, self, and consciousness emerge as concepts evolved from social interaction.[22] According to this line of reasoning, a person *needs to communicate* with others in order to verify his own view of himself. However, if there is considerable question in our mind about our social capabilities, we are not likely to expose ourselves via communication with others. In fact, we will likely *fear* communication situations. Research evidence tends to support this line of reasoning.[23]

Both Heider's balance theory and Festinger's theory of cognitive

---

[21]For a detailed discussion of the personality characteristics related to speech anxiety (self-concept, need for achievement, and general anxiety tendency) see K. Giffin and K. Bradley, "Group Counseling for Speech Students with Low Self-Confidence: An Approach and a Rationale," *Journal of Communication, 19* (1969), 22–29. Also see K. Giffin *et al., A Correlational Study of Self-Image, Speech Anxiety, and Trust of Others,* Research Report R/24, Lawrence, Kans., Communication Research Center, Univ. of Kansas, 1970.

[22]C. H. Cooley, *Social Organization,* New York, Scribner's 1909. Also see G. H. Mead, *Mind, Self and Society,* Chicago, Univ. of Chicago Press, 1934.

[23]H. Gilkinson, "A Questionnaire Study of the Causes of Social Fears Among College Speech Students," *Speech Monographs, 10* (1943), 74–83. Also E. Bormann and G. Shapiro, "Perceived Confidence as a Function of Self-Image," *Central States Speech Journal, 13* (1962), 253–256.

NEXT I GOT MYSELF A CAT WHO WAS VERY WITHDRAWN AT FIRST.

BUT I TRAINED MY CAT TO TRUST ME, TO LOVE ME, TO COME ANYTIME I CALLED.

NOW I LIVE CONTENTEDLY WITH MY PARAKEET, MY DOG AND MY CAT. WE SPEND EVERY MINUTE OF THE DAY LEARNING TO RELATE. IT'S BEEN AN INVALUABLE EXPERIENCE.

PRETTY SOON I'LL BE READY FOR PEOPLE.

dissonance would lead us to suspect that a person with a very high concept of self would not fear exposure in his interaction with others, and even if an attack upon his self-image occurred, he would likely disparage the source of the attack. Very likely he would filter such information, accepting only that which tended to agree with (confirm) it. Exactly the same reasoning would lead us to suspect that *a person with a low concept of self would accept information which confirms his low opinion of himself and reject information which would tend to raise it.* There is research support for this line of reasoning. Bergin has demonstrated that when (1) a person's self-concept is low, and (2) the information received from another person is favorable about his behavior, he will tend to resolve this dissonance by discrediting the source.[24] An experiment by Deutsch and Solomon indicated that persons with low concept of self will tend to filter and accept information congruent with their concept; such subjects viewed *low* evaluations of themselves from others more favorably than they viewed high self-evaluations.[25]

In our culture having a low concept of self is not a pleasant experience. Confirmation of it, even if such is valid, is likewise not pleasant. Thus, the individual with low self-esteem will pay more attention to information which confirms his low concept, but not be happy about it. He actually *fears* confirmation of his fears. In terms of interpersonal relationships, the protection of one's self-image is closely linked with trust of those with whom one interacts. Self-confidence in interpersonal relations can be conceptualized as willingness to expose one's self-concept to evaluation by others.

In a summary of the literature on the self-concept, Roger Brown concludes that there is a strong relationship between a broad conception of oneself and one's conception of others with whom one interacts (or, if I like people, I tend to like me.)[26] Rogers has argued that when an individual interacts with trusted others, he is then able to *form* new and more favorable perceptions of himself; that is, he

[24]A. E. Bergin, "The Effects of Dissonant Persuasive Communications upon Changes in a Self-Referring Attitude," *Journal of Personality, 30* (1962), 423–438.

[25]M. Deutsch and L. Solomon, "Reactions to Evaluations by Others as Influenced by Self-Evaluations," *Sociometry, 22* (1959), 93–112.

[26]R. Brown, *Social Psychology,* New York, Free Press, 1965, p. 650.

can come to afford exposure of his self-concept for possible self-reevaluation.[27] In his later work, *On Becoming a Person,* Rogers presents considerable evidence that exposure of oneself is accomplished only when a person trusts his listener.[28] Thus we may posit the principle that self-confidence in interpersonal communication is a function of trust of the other person in any given communication situation.

There is evidence that we tend to extend trust to another person when we perceive him as (1) in possession of viable (useful to us) information or knowledge, (2) reliable in terms of our goal-aspirations, (3) and dynamic, *i.e.,* active rather than passive.[29] A communicator tends to trust a *listener* when he perceives these characteristics in the listener. Pursuing this line of reasoning we find the following generalizations tenable: (1) self-confidence in a given interpersonal communication situation is a function of *perceived ability* of others *to understand intended messages:* this perceived ability is related to the degree of their pertinent knowledge and/or information; (2) self-confidence in a given interpersonal communication situation is a function of *perceived reliability* of the others present *regarding one's communication objectives* in that situation; and (3) self-confidence in a given interpersonal situation is a function of the degree of *perceived dynamism* of the others present.

In view of the findings cited above, the following principles may be stated: (1) self-confidence in a given interpersonal communication situation is a function of perceived *acceptance* by valued others; and (2) there is an interaction between three types of trust, all three of which are functionally related to self-confidence in a given interpersonal communication situation: (a) trust of oneself, (b) trust extended *toward* others, and (c) perceived evidence of trust extended *by* others.

## Increasing One's Trust of Others

If speech anxiety and one's tendency toward withdrawal from communication situations are related to his trust of others, it is a natural question to ask: how can one's trust of others be increased?

[27]Rogers, *Client-Centered Therapy, op. cit.,* pp. 515–524.
[28]Rogers, *On Becoming a Person, op. cit.,* pp. 39–58.
[29]Giffin, "The Contribution of Studies of Source Credibility," *op. cit.,* 104–120.

There is some evidence that people who are more successful socially (i.e., get along well with others) are more trustful of others.[30]

It should be acknowledged that in some cases, increasing a person's trust of others may be dangerous; some dupes are altogether too trusting. However, if a person is abnormally distrustful of other persons, that is, if he has unrealistic or irrational fear of others in social or communicative situations, then attempts on his part to increase his general level of trust of other people seems warranted. By achieving a more objective perception of others he can hope to raise his own self-concept and reduce his speech anxiety.[31] But how can one's trust of others be increased?

Interpersonal trust can best be achieved in a climate of *perceived acceptance* of the individual by others with whom he interacts. Personal change in a socially desirable way—and in a way desirable for the individual—requires a climate of acceptance and support. This climate of acceptance is sometimes found in T-groups (sensitivity training groups) and in therapy groups. From his work with normal subjects who were attempting to change their own personality dimensions in order to make their interpersonal relations more effective, Gibb has drawn the following conclusion:

*A person learns to grow through his increasing acceptance of himself and others. Serving as the primary block to such acceptance are the defensive feelings of fear and distrust that arise from the prevailing defensive climates in most cultures. In order to participate consciously in his own growth, a person must learn to create for himself, in his dyadic and group relationships, defensive-reductive climates that will continue to reduce his own fears and distrusts.*[32]

It seems somewhat obvious that a key variable in increasing a person's trust of others is the behavior of those others. Studies of counselors, summarized by Truax and Carkhuff, indicate variation in the relationship between counselors and clients. Specifically, counselors vary as to characteristics of *accurate empathy, nonpossessive*

[30]Giffin *et al., op. cit.*
[31]See evidence cited by K. Giffin and M. Heider, "A Theory of the Relationship Between Speech Anxiety and the Suppression of Communication in Childhood," *Psychiatric Quarterly Supplement,* 2 (1967), 311–322.
[32]Gibb, "Climate for Trust Formation," *op. cit.,* p. 279.

*warmth,* and *genuineness.* A large number of studies cited in this review have demonstrated that counselors who show above-average amounts of empathy, warmth, and genuineness have above-average success with psychoneurotic clients in psychiatric hospitals, psychiatric outpatient clinics, veterans clinics, college counseling centers, and juvenile delinquency institutions. These studies include both individual and group counseling approaches.[33]

The following line of reasoning thus emerges: (1) speech anxiety involves low concept of self and distrust of others; (2) irrational distrust of others is significantly reduced by interaction with therapists and counselors who show empathy, warmth, and genuineness; thus the inference—an environment which can measurably reduce speech anxiety is one in which a person is shown high degrees of these elements of rapport.

This inference makes logical sense: an anxious person can cope more easily with a communication environment in which he receives empathy, warmth, and genuineness. Successful coping with this communication environment may provide additional interpersonal confidence.

## DEFENSIVE COMMUNICATION

The reverse of trusting communication behavior is defensiveness. The basic cause of defensiveness is inherent in one's unmet interpersonal needs. We need supportive feedback from valued others to achieve a satisfactory self-image. When this need remains unmet a general feeling of anxiety is produced. Unresolved anxiety generates defensive tactics when we are with other people. Defensive behavior simply may be a show of fear, including postural, facial, or verbal signals that warn the other person to be careful. Or our defensive behavior may involve small signs of our desire to withdraw—verbal hesitancies, stepping backward, turning sideways, or simply paying more attention to some other person. These defensive behaviors are real, and not very devious; thus, the other person can respond to them directly as signs of anxiety or fear.

[33]C. B. Truax and R. R. Carkhuff, *Toward Effective Counseling and Psychotherapy,* Chicago, Aldine, 1967.

From *The Unexpurgated Memoirs of Bernard Mergendeiler,* by Jules Feiffer. Copyright © 1959, 1961, 1962, 1963, 1964, 1965 by Jules Feiffer. Reprinted by permission of Random House, Inc.

A more disagreeable strategy of defensiveness is the deliberate distortion of the message received. All of us have heard exchanges such as the following: (She) "Will you please shut the door; I feel cold." (He) "Why don't you just say you don't want me coming in and bothering you?"

A most serious form of defensive strategy is direct, personal attack. A severe problem arises when the person attacked is unaware that in some way he is perceived as a threat; in such a case he will likely view the attack as pure, unprovoked aggression.[34] A brief example may serve to illustrate the complexity of this type of behavior. Recently one of our students, a coed, went home to visit her parents who were having marital strife. Approximately at the time of her arrival her mother was "leaving," to go to her mother's home. The mother asked the girl to go with her, and upon their arrival at the grandmother's home, the girl telephoned her father that they had arrived safely. Her mother asked her why she had done so; the girl replied, "I knew he would be worried." Her mother accused, "Why have you turned against me?" In talking about the incident, the girl interpreted her mother's attack as unprovoked aggression, although she made some allowance for her highly emotional condition at that time. Even so, her resentment of her mother's attack was clearly unresolved.

## Communication Behavior Which Stimulates Defensiveness

Sometimes we find ourselves in a defensive posture without quite knowing how it came about. Knowledge about communication behavior tending to produce or increase defensiveness may help us forestall our signal reactions of defensiveness. Investigation of such incidents has identified the following contributory conditions, or causes, of defensive behavior:

1. *Evaluation* by expression, manner of speech, tone of voice, or verbal content, perceived by the receiver (listener) as criticism or judgment, will produce defensive behavior.
2. Communication perceived by the recipient as an attempt to *control* him will produce defensiveness; it is very interesting to

[34]P. Watzlawick, J. H. Beavin, and D. D. Jackson, *Pragmatics of Human Communication*, New York, Norton, 1967, pp. 80–93.

note that if speech can be said to be a social "tool," the implication is that the recipient has been "tooled."
3. *Strategems* which are perceived as clever devices produce defensiveness; partially hidden motives breed suspicion. Persons seen as "playing a game," feigning emotion, withholding information, or having private *access* to sources of data, will stimulate defensive responses.
4. An appearance of *lack of concern* for the welfare of a person will heighten his need for defensiveness. Such "neutrality" may be necessary at times, but people strongly need to be perceived as valued persons. A clinically detached or impersonal manner (not caring) is usually feared and resented.
5. An attitude of *superiority* arouses defensive behavior; any behavior which reinforces the recipient's feelings of inadequacy is a source of disturbance.
6. *Dogmatism* is a well-known stimulus of defensive behavior; if you know something "for certain," it is wise to determine whether or not anyone else wants to hear it from you, and whether they want your answer to be offered tentatively or with final certainty.[35]

## Requisite Conditions for Reducing Defensive Behavior

About a quarter of a century ago Carl Rogers began to report a movement toward a nondirective approach to psychotherapy. These practices culminated in his client-centered approach. The relevant point here is his emphasis on the patient's need for personal trust in the therapist and his communication behavior. Rogers emphasized acceptance or *psychological safety* in psychotherapy groups.[36]

Rogers' approach was a forerunner of Gibb's concept of *supportive climate* in the communication process.[37] Starting a long-range research effort in 1953 Jack Gibb focused his efforts upon the reduction of defensive behavior in groups. This defensive behavior seemed to be caused, in part, by lack of interpersonal trust. In later work he began to focus on trust and its development, associating trust with

[35]Gibb, "Defensive Communication," *op. cit.,* 146–148.
[36]Rogers, *Client-Centered Therapy, op. cit.,* pp. 515–520.
[37]Gibb, "Defensive Communication," *op. cit.,* 143.

interpersonal acceptance.[38] According to his findings, defensive behavior is reduced by interaction that is perceived by the individual as
(1) descriptive rather than evaluative or critical; (2) oriented toward
solving of mutual problems rather than oriented toward personal
control; (3) spontaneous rather than strategic; (4) empathic rather than
neutral; (5) indicative of an attitude of equality instead of superiority;
and (6) expressive of provisionally held viewpoints instead of dogmatic certainties.[39] Additional studies by Gibb tend to corroborate
these findings.[40]

### Effects of Reducing Defensiveness

As interpersonal trust is increased, interpersonal relationships
are changed so that there is (1) increased acceptance of legitimate
influence by others; (2) decreased suspicion of motives of others; (3)
increased tolerance for deviant behavior of others; (4) increased stability when one is not trusted by others; (5) shifting of emphasis to
control over group interaction process rather than control over individuals; and (6) further increases in interpersonal trust.[41]

Changes in personality characteristics are not easy to produce;
changes in behavior which seem to indicate changes in personality
structure may be only temporary. Even so, studies tend to indicate
that, as defensive behavior decreases and interpersonal trust increases,
two very important personality changes can occur: (1) we tend to
achieve heightened feelings of personal adequacy (improved self-
image); and (2) we achieve easier acceptance of our temporary feelings of internal conflict (less anxiety).[42] Reducing defensive behavior
and increasing interpersonal trust appear to be extremely valuable
goals in terms of effective interpersonal communication.

## "GAPS" BETWEEN PEOPLE

Dwight D. Eisenhower is said to have typified the simple virtues
of the heartland of his nation. Even so, as he saw it, the most im-

[38]Gibb, "Climate for Trust Formation," op. cit., p. 290.
[39]Gibb, "Defensive Communication," op. cit., 612.
[40]J. Gibb, "Dynamics of Leadership," Current Issues of Higher Education, Washington, D. C., American Association for Higher Education, 1967.
[41]Giffin, "Interpersonal Trust in Small-Group Communication," op. cit.
[42]Ibid.

portant message he could leave with the people of his boyhood "hometown," was that not even the people of Abilene, Kansas, could ever again afford to think that the way in which people thought and acted in other parts of the world would not directly influence their lives. A most significant problem today is that of overcoming communication barriers between different groups and groupings of people. Gaps need to be bridged between members of different reference groups, different generations, and different cultures and minority subcultures.

## Barriers Between Members of Different Reference Groups

In order to be adequate socially we must achieve personal beliefs, attitudes, and convictions which help us to function well with those people who surround us. Conflicts over norms of behavior and belief usually prove to be quite threatening. If our personal standards and norms seriously conflict with those of people in our immediate environment, the experience is likely to be painful because our very basis of existence is at stake.

When we identify with a group such as the people in our community we almost inevitably adopt and defend the standards and behavior of that group. A group with which we thus identify is sometimes called a "reference group."

To think well of ourselves it is necessary to think well of those with whom we identify, i.e., our reference group. This process of identification introduces a certain degree of narrowness or distortion in our perceptual field; this limiting and distorting of our perception of "foreigners" (persons not in our reference group) then becomes a major source of breakdown in communication.

Since each of us accepts our own perceptions as "reality," the customs and attitudes of our reference group are judged to be superior when they are different from those of other groups. Other people and other groups are then judged according to these standards. Americans commonly place a high value upon houses with modern plumbing. As a result, many American soldiers consider that the Germans are superior to the French. If you say, "Well, they are!" then you have illustrated the point at issue—you have made a judgment based upon a standard derived from your American reference group.

The boy George, who has identified with a predelinquent gang, has a different system of prestige values from Charles, who has identified with the Boy Scouts. Not only do the two boys admire different institutions, but different individuals and types of "success." It is not enough to say that they "don't talk the same language"—such may be the case, and if so, communication is hampered. But even if they know and agree on the same meanings for words, their system of values is different; Charles will think the predelinquent boy is wrong, and that boy will judge Charles to be naive and ignorant. This kind of problem is not uncommon; in fact, two such boys may even live within the same city block. Even so, bridging the communication gap in this rather common setting is not at all easy.

In the larger social sense, the insular thinking described above is one of the principal barriers to intercultural cooperation. People of almost all cultures sincerely desire a better world and a better society; the barrier consists of lack of agreement among the various groups as to what constitutes a good society. Members of each culture consider their own version of society as fundamentally right because it (more or less) satisfies their personal needs as they see them. Thus, they believe that the better society can only arise from a further development and modification of their own. This is true for Iranians, Hindus, Berbers, Eskimos, Russians, and Americans.[43] When members of different reference groups or subcultures try to communicate, it frequently seems that their actions are chiefly intended to hinder or obstruct another group's efforts to create their version of a "better" world.

How can such gaps ever be bridged? In a way, every individual bridges a similar gap whenever he tries to contact and "get to know" any other single individual. We start by accepting and even adopting a few behaviors of others which help us to satisfy some personal need. As we accept or adopt behaviors, we later modify our attitudes, beliefs, and value systems. For example, the white man's alcohol was a boon from heaven in the eyes of the Plains Indians who viewed the world as a place where man became great ("successful") and held power over others through dreams and delirium. On the other hand, the Hopi, living in a world of fragile order and regularity,

---

[43] A. W. Combs and D. Snygg, *Individual Behavior*, rev. ed., New York, Harper & Row, 1959, pp. 341–344.

where a small mistake could bring personal hardship, saw alcohol as a great menace and rejected it.

This process of acceptance of the ways, attitudes, and beliefs of others is speeded up if the other person has some acceptable source of status, or if the behavior satisfies some immediate and important personal need.[44] New ways of doing things which otherwise fit our customary pattern of behavior are easily accepted and adopted. Once the change is made, we quickly find additional reasons why it was a good idea; thus we reduce the cognitive dissonance imposed by the new behavior.[45]

The primary tool in this process of bridging gaps between reference groups is, of course, getting them to look at each other without perceptual distortion. The real barrier is the a priori notion that just because a person is a member of another group his behavior and his beliefs will doubtless be full of mistakes (inferior). People who fail to conform to our standards tend to be viewed as ignorant or evil or both. Such prejudgment—judgment without taking an objective, open-minded, inquisitive look to see first and judge later— is properly called prejudice. People of no nation, religion, or smaller group have been entirely free of this problem. Even a teacher, who ordinarily is a severe critic of his own educational system, will have difficulty giving objective consideration to the suggestions of those who are not a part of the system. However, such objectivity is the true basis of tolerance and makes possible the bridging of gaps between members of different reference groups.

## The Generation Gap

For most of the twentieth century there have usually been identifiable differences between the folkways, attitudes, and beliefs of two consecutive generations; technological advances in machines, factories, automobiles, telephones, etc., have produced differences in ways of communicating and interacting with others. However, the cultural gap today between persons in their forties and beyond and those in their twenties is much greater than in previous times. This is true for two reasons.

[44]R. Linton, The Cultural Background of Personality, New York, Appleton-Century-Crofts, 1945, pp. 39–74.
[45]S. Feldman, Cognitive Consistency, New York, Academic Press, 1966, pp. 43–57.

In the first place, technological advancement has a way of self-accelerating; each single advancement paves the way for a number of new developments, until the speed of additional technological changes is tremendous. We have reached the point in this change process where for those of us who are forty, very little happened in the first twenty years of our lives which prepared us very well for the last twenty. In fact, much of what we did then is now outmoded.

The second reason for the current generation gap is the advent of the "affluent society." The so-called Protestant ethic, the idea that work is good and leisurely idleness is bad, served a frontier society very well. Today the need for it does not seem critical. As the authors of this book work overtime in its preparation, the children of one of the authors say, "Dad, you don't need to work that hard; it'll be all right. Come on and go to the movies with us—we have the money!" And of course they do—they always have more cash than their Dad.

We could well afford to take our technological advances and enjoy them; we could accept our young folks' advice and relax our way of life. Many members of the younger generation are sincerely questioning attitudes and beliefs generally accepted by the older one: issues of social justice versus law and order, and social welfare versus capitalism. In addition, the problem described in the previous section traps us: each generation is convinced that the folkways and value system of the other is in error. We focus on the differences and ignore the similarities; we see only beards and sandals or bald heads and worried frowns.

The writers of this book are convinced that there is a strong, abiding ethic in our American culture that will keep us from letting the generation gap become a severe social problem—it is simply this: the American people have throughout their history had a strong regard for the value of the individual person. Our most severe national crises have each been settled with a favorable consideration of this principle. Perhaps we should all remember that when someone makes his plea to be allowed just to "do his thing"—grow a beard, wear ragged jeans, or work at night trying to write a book—he is simply asking for an ancient American privilege—to be himself as an unhampered individual. As suggested in the section above, an open-minded objective look at a person of the "other generation" can be the start toward bridging the generation gap on an interpersonal level.

## Gaps between Cultures and Minority Subcultures

We have been vaguely aware of the problem of communication between segments of cultures or subcultures ever since it was discovered in Boston that Lowells talked only to Cabots and Cabots talked only to God. Today, the need for communication between members of different subcultures is more urgent. Our primary concern in this section is with interpersonal communication barriers between representatives of different cultures or subcultures; such problems are brought to light at the "interface" between cultural groups.

Communities that pride themselves on tolerance and absence of prejudice almost always have only a few members of a minority group in their midst. Minority groups become threatening to majority groups only when they are large or powerful. When a group feels threatened its members tend to accentuate or idealize the reference group's characteristics. Examples of this behavior are the great upsurge of Zionism after the Nazi atrocities and the current glorification of color in the Negro press.

When individuals are threatened, two negative effects upon their perceptual processes occur: (1) their perceptions tend to be narrowed to the object of threat so that it is difficult to see broadly and clearly, and (2) they tend to be much more rigidly defensive of their existing perceptions.[46]

As a general principle, the psychological effects of intergroup threat or conflict are felt at the lower socioeconomic levels of these groups, especially if persons at these lower levels are the victims of domination or aggression within their own group.[47] For example, in our own South, the most violent reactions to school integration have occurred among the "poor white" lower economic classes.

That point of greatest potential for bridging intercultural gaps is at the interface between the cultures, i.e., the personal, face-to-face

[46]Combs and Snygg, op. cit., pp. 165–189.
[47]D. Snygg, "The Relative Difficulty of Mechanically Equivalent Tasks: I. Human Learning," Journal of Genetic Psychology, 47 (1935), 299–320.

interaction between official and unofficial representatives of those cultures. Such persons are generally better educated, more broadly experienced and feel less personally threatened by representatives of the other culture.

At this interface a common language capability is helpful but not the major problem. For example, in the earlier periods of World War II, American soldiers and Russian soldiers found ways of easily overcoming the language problem. The need for action in a common cause made individuals from the different cultures important to each other; there was even a certain pleasure in getting acquainted with new allies—Americans were pleasantly surprised at the great physical stamina and courage of the Russian soldier.

What is severely needed by intercultural representatives at this interface is objectivity of perception, as suggested in previous sections. Intercultural conflict is always carried on by individuals who think of their antagonists as *members of the other group* rather than as individual human beings. Intergroup conflict at the cultural interface can be diminished by increasing the capability of the representative members to differentiate one another as individuals.[48]

Increased interaction between such representatives is helpful; it fosters the capability of these persons to see each other as individuals rather than as "Blacks" or "Whites," German or Jews, Russians or Americans.[49] A very interesting procedure developed by R. D. DuBois has been shown to be an effective means of promoting better relationships between such representatives of different groups. Instead of talking about intergroup or intercultural problems and differences, they are asked to talk about pleasant childhood memories.[50] Members of both groups talk about their experiences in smelling and tasting enjoyable foods, playing games, and participating in athletic events. After a while, they feel as if they have had similar experiences, somewhat similar childhoods, and are first of all members of the

[48]B. Kutner, C. Wilkins, and P. Yarrow, "Verbal Attitudes and Overt Behavior Involving Racial Prejudice," *Journal of Abnormal and Social Psychology*, 47 (1952), 649–652.

[49]J. W. Thibaut and J. Coules, "The Role of Communication in the Reduction of Interpersonal Hostility," *Journal of Abnormal and Social Psychology*, 47 (1952), 770–777.

[50]R. D. DuBois, *Get Together, Americans*, New York, Harper & Row, 1943.

common human race. Shared experiences make possible a common feeling; further, shared experiences provide a more personal, human view of a member of another group or culture.

The objective view of one another, a view which is focused on the other person as an individual human being rather than a specimen of a strange cultural type, is the basis for effective interpersonal communication between intercultural representatives. Such effective communication behavior is highly useful in reducing intergroup conflict for the following reasons: (1) it maximizes human capability for tolerance of differences and acceptance of new or different folkways and attitudes; and (2) it minimizes the degree of fear and feelings of threat imposed by the other group, race, or culture.

## FEELINGS OF ALIENATION

In comments on current social problems the term "alienation" is frequently used. Sometimes these comments are about the "alienated teen-ager" or the "alienated generation." There are many persons in our society who appear to hold negative attitudes toward other persons in their immediate social environment. For this reason, the problem deserves special consideration.

In common parlance the term "alienated" usually refers to persons who are estranged or withdrawn from other persons with whom they would ordinarily be expected to associate, to admire, or even to love. A student who has turned away from his teachers, that is, who has ceased to talk with them in the way that they expect or desire, sometimes may be called "alienated." When a whole generation "under thirty" appears to be distrustful of all persons "over thirty," it is time to look carefully at the possible causes.

### Problem of the Alienated Person

The term "alienated" has two usages pertinent to our discussion. The first simply refers to a person who withdraws from or avoids another person or persons. This withdrawal behavior has been identified as *social alienation,* and is defined by Hajda, a representative authority in this area, as follows.

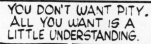

*Alienation is an individual's feeling of uneasiness or discomfort which reflects his exclusion or self-exclusion from social and cultural participation. It is an expression of non-belonging or non-sharing, an uneasy awareness or perception of unwelcome contrast with others. It varies in scope and intensity. It may be restricted to a few limited situations, such as participation in a peer group, or it may encompass a wide social universe, including participation in the larger society . . . in this sense, alienation is a general social phenomenon, a feeling that may be experienced in some fashion by any member of a given society. It cannot be understood apart from its opposite, the feeling of belonging, sharing, or participation which follows from the individual's inclusion or integration into the social collectivities.*[51]

Although we will here be using the term "alienation" to refer to *social* alienation (avoidance or withdrawal behavior) it should be noted that common usage of the term connotes an implication of mental disturbance. This connotation comes from the technical use of the term in psychiatry. Hinsie and Campbell in their *Psychiatric Dictionary* give the psychological definition of *mental alienation* as follows:

*The repression, inhibition, blocking or dissociation of one's own feelings so that they no longer seem effective, familiar, or convincing to the patient.*[52]

Thus, whenever a person is said to be alienated there is a connotative suggestion of personal maladjustment.

Alienation does not mean simple disagreement with another person, even if the disagreement is violent, *so long as interaction continues.* When one *cannot communicate* with another person or persons and *withdraws from interaction,* alienation, in the sense we are using the term, has occurred. In this way one can become alienated from a person or a group—a brother, sister, mother, father, husband, wife, teacher, peer group, school, reference group, or even an entire

[51]J. Hajda, "Alienation and Integration of Student Intellectuals," *American Sociological Review,* 26 (1961), 758–759.
[52]L. E. Hinsie and R. J. Campbell, *Psychiatric Dictionary,* 3d ed., New York, Oxford Univ. Press, 1960, p. 26.

culture or social system. Alienation thus involves a conclusion that one's attempts to communicate with a person (or persons) are pointless. At this point functional withdrawal from interaction begins.

Alienation of a person toward another can be partial; one can be convinced that he will be denied the opportunity for communication on certain topics or at certain times or under certain conditions. As long as he is allowed to communicate on most topics most of the time, the degree of alienation is only slight. The severity of alienation increases as a person perceives an increase in the relative number of times or topics on which his communication is denied.

Alienation can occur between a person and one or more others. Complete alienation toward one other person may not matter very much; complete or nearly complete alienation between a person and many others can make his life miserable. William James once said, "No more fiendish punishment could be devised, even were such a thing physically possible, than that one should be turned loose in society and remain absolutely unnoticed by all the members thereof."[53]

Alienation does not occur between a person and someone whom he has never known. It does occur most noticeably when a person withdraws from interaction with someone he has known well or ought to know well, such as a parent, wife, or husband.

As described above, alienation from another person does not mean neurotic behavior: when confronted with denial of one's attempts to communicate, it is perfectly rational to conclude (1) "He won't talk with me (on those topics, now, or under those conditions)" or (2) "It is not worth my time to try to talk with him (on those topics, now, or under those conditions)." Neurotic alienation begins when reality is ignored, that is, when the above conclusions are drawn in the face of identifiable evidence to the contrary. It becomes critical when a person denies his feelings which are at the same time expressed in obvious behavioral ways.

Our primary interest here is in social alienation, that is, in the breakdown of an interpersonal relationship which is ordinarily expected by society to be stable and beneficial, such as the relationship between a child and his parents or teachers.

[53]Quoted by R. D. Laing, *The Self and Others; Further Studies in Sanity and Madness*, London, Tavistock, 1961, p. 89.

Of course, such social alienation does not meet the criteria for mental alienation given. However, it is sometimes viewed by parents and even by others in society as mental disturbance. This confusion in thinking occurs as follows: (1) the socially alienated person may appear to his parents to be repressing, inhibiting, blocking, or denying his *expected or desired* warm feelings about them, and (2) these expected or desired feelings no longer seem to be operative in producing "appropriate" responses to the overtures of the parents.

This breakdown of such a relationship can be analyzed in terms of communication theory; that is, it constitutes a refusal to utilize a communication channel which is generally thought to be available and useful. An important question for the student of communication behavior is thus exposed: What kinds of communication behavior tend to produce alienation?

Tangential questions are the following: Is it possible that "the alienated" are realistically responding to communication events in an intelligent way? Can such alienating communication events be described in a way that will provide insight and understanding of this socially relevant problem? Are "the alienated" mistakenly withdrawing from social interaction which would be very useful to them? Or have parents or teachers or other important persons unknowingly or thoughtlessly provided excellent causes for such social withdrawal?

An exploratory study of this problem is being made through analyses of interviews with college students who appear to be alienated from teachers and peer groups. The data tend to indicate that certain prior communication events have transpired. These events can be identified as misuse or misunderstanding of one or more of the basic principles of interpersonal communication suggested in Chapter 1. We will give this problem detailed consideration here because we have found that young people of our acquaintance are very much concerned about it.

## Communication Principles Related to Social Alienation

It has been our experience that understanding of the ways in which basic principles of interpersonal communication may be ignored or violated can lead to a better understanding of one's feelings of alienation. In addition, such insights can provide the basis for changes in one's communication behavior that may lead to the reduction of the feeling of alienation. Your own insights and your changes in use of interpersonal communication techniques may or may not change the behavior of those persons from whom you feel alienated, but such additional insight can at least help you to understand yourself and others better.

The first of these principles was simply stated: *we communicate on two levels.* The first level is that of message-sending; the second level is that of providing information about the message, that is, metacommunication. When the message itself is in conflict with or contradictory to the metacommunication *about* the message, a natural response is confusion and at least a partial attempt at withdrawal from further interaction. If parents say, "We really do love you, John," but say it in a way which shows distrust, suspicion, fear, anger, or hostility, social alienation is a reasonable result from John's point of view.

The second principle of interpersonal communication which appears to be related to alienation is this: *in an interpersonal situation one cannot refuse to communicate.* A refusal to interact with another person is a communication in and of itself. When another person simply refuses to talk to you (perhaps for a reason thought to be excellent by that person) the message given to you is conclusive: they do not *wish* to talk with you. Such a conclusion provides an excellent reason for withdrawal from later interaction when it is not absolutely necessary.

The third related principle is that *nonverbal metacommunication ultimately establishes the nature of an interpersonal relationship.* Many times we actually receive verbal messages from another person telling us how they perceive our interpersonal relationship with them: "I like to be with you"; or "I enjoy talking with you." Sometimes we believe what we hear; however, if the other person's nonverbal behavior is in conflict with such a verbal message, we usually recall the old adage that "actions speak louder than words." In the final analysis, a person's perception of his relationship with another is determined by the latter's nonverbal metacommunication. In many interviews we have been told by students that "my parents said they loved me, but they didn't act like it." Such behavior appears to us to be reasonable justification for diminishing interaction.

The fourth related principle is that *the degree to which two persons similarly perceive their relationship will heavily influence the interpretation of communication between the two.* Different perceptions of their relationship by two persons can lead to serious and even violent disagreement between them regarding what one has really "said" to the other. There is a case study of the husband and wife who frequently participated in violent quarrels. An example occurred one day when the husband received a phone call from a friend who was in town for a few days. The husband immediately invited the friend to stay at their home when he arrived in town. When he told his wife, a bitter quarrel arose over the desirable and undesirable characteristics of this friend. Finally, the wife agreed that an invitation to the friend was the appropriate and natural thing, but concluded with this comment: "Well, you may be right, but you are wrong because you are arguing with me." In actual fact the real conflict was over the husband's right to take such initiative without consulting his wife; this concerned their perceptions of the nature of their interpersonal relationship. In their quarrel this couple committed a very common mistake in their communication. They argued about the characteristics of a third person while actually disagreeing about their treatment of each other, failing completely to resolve the confusion between their two perceptions of their own interpersonal relationship.[54]

At this point we can briefly summarize the potential impact of the four basic principles of interpersonal communication given: *in an interpersonal situation, nonverbal metacommunication usually establishes the nature of an interpersonal relationship, which in turn heavily influences interpretations of both communication and metacommunication by both persons in the relationship.*

### Alienation by Communication Denial

The initiation of any communication (including metacommunication) carries with it an implied request: "Please validate me." This plea can be in the form of a request for recognition of one's ideas as worthwhile; even in such a case, however, there is an obvious implication regarding the value of oneself personally. Note that in an interpersonal situation we *cannot refuse* to respond to such a

[54]Watzlawick *et al., op. cit.,* pp. 80–81.

request—an attempt to avoid giving a response provides denial, a special problem to be discussed below.

There are three ways in which a person can respond to the implied request for validation of another person: (1) agreement—a person or his idea is responded to as somewhat worthwhile or valid; (2) disagreement—the person or his idea is responded to as more or less invalid; and (3) denial of the existence of the question. This denial (that is, an attempt to refuse to give any response at all) not only denies the existence of the question, "please validate me," but by implication denies the existence of the other person on a functional, interpersonal, or communicational level. This point is somewhat complex and deserves at least brief explanation.

Little Johnnie, age five, comes home from kindergarten and says, "I have a girl friend." His mother says, "Eat your soup, Johnnie." This constitutes a denial of Johnnie's capability of discussing girl friends (at that time)—perhaps an event of no great consequence. Ten years later John says "Dad, Joe Smith is taking his folks' car to the school picnic Saturday." Dad says, "Finish your homework, John." This is an example of a denial of John's right to talk about using the family car, that is, a denial of John's existence on this communicational level. Two such instances in ten years is inconsequential; two instances per day for ten years is another matter. Also, denial of communication on one isolated topic may not pose a severe threat to an individual's self-validation. Remember, however, that the question of his validity is implied with every statement John ever makes and that in any interpersonal situation the other person cannot refuse to respond to it: a refusal becomes at least a temporary or partial denial of John's self-identity.

The impact of such denial depends upon the value a person places upon the other person or persons, or perhaps upon the value he places upon his relationship with them. Consistent and continued denial of a child by his parents can work severe damage. Ronald Laing of the Tavistock Institute of Human Relations in London has given the following description of what happens when a child is denied in this manner:

> The characteristic family pattern that has emerged from the study of families of schizophrenics does not so much involve

*a child who is subject to outright neglect or even to obvious trauma, but a child whose authenticity has been subjected to subtle, but persistent, mutilation, often quite unwittingly.*[55]

In another paragraph Laing poignantly describes the effect on the child:

*The ultimate of this is . . . no matter how a person feels or how he acts, no matter what meaning he gives his situations, his feelings are denuded of validity, his acts are stripped of their motives, intentions and consequences; the situation is robbed of its meaning for him so that he is totally mystified and alienated.*[56]

In commenting on our society Martin Buber wrote as follows:

*At all its levels, persons confirm one another in a practical way, to some extent or other, in their personal qualities and capacities, and the society may be termed human in the measure to which its members confirm one another . . . The basis of man's life with man is two-fold and it is one; the wish of every man to be confirmed as what he is even as what he can become, by men, and the innate capacity of man to confirm his fellow men in this way; that this capacity lies so immeasurably fallow constitutes the real weakness and questionableness of the human race; actual humanity exists only where this capacity unfolds.*[57]

We should note that the implied request, "Validate me," may be put by an individual, a group, a subculture, or even a nation; also the responses—agreement, disagreement, or denial of existence—may be made by another individual, a group, a subculture, or a nation. Perhaps not in the last year, but certainly in previous years, most of us have seen an adult black person attempt to ask a sincere, intelligent question about how to perform a part of his job, only to be given a response of this order: "Boy, bring me that board over there!" Looking backward, it seems to the present writers that much of the

---

[55]Laing, *op. cit.*, p. 91.
[56]*Ibid.*, pp. 135–136.
[57]M. Buber, "Distance and Relation," *Psychiatry, 20* (1957), 97–104.

observed communication of white people with black people has carried a denial of the latters' capability to interact with others as worthwhile human beings.

There are two major ways in which an individual can respond to the denial described: (1) he can refuse to accept it as a denial, or (2) he can accept the idea that he does not exist on that communication level. Communication behaviors exhibiting a refusal to accept such a denial include (1) repetition of the request, (2) escalation of the tone or manner of the request, and (3) overt verbal metacommunication about the denial.

Repetition of the request simply involves continuation of any verbal communication with its attendant implied request, "Please validate me." Escalation can involve changes in vocal tone or intensity, threatening posture, violent gestures, or on a larger scale, demonstrations, riots, etc. Overt metacommunication likely would look something like this: "Dad, why don't you talk with me about my using the family car on the picnic?" It should be noted that such overt metacommunication is rarely initiated by the person in the weaker, "one-down" position who feels threatened, and, of course, such denial of one's existence (on any level) by a valued other will produce a feeling of threat.[58]

Acceptance of the implication of denial of oneself is more common than many people believe; many persons accept the idea that they are unworthy of talking to "better" people, people with more influence, more education, more experience or just more self-assurance. This phenomenon is not really uncommon. The acceptance of this implication is frequently a constituent of the process of social alienation.[59]

A particularly interesting problem arises when communication denial occurs and at the same time the denied person cannot withdraw from a situation because of the value he places on a potential relationship with that specific other person. In an analysis of the communication environment of schizophrenia, Bateson and his associates[60] coined the term "double bind" to identify a communication situation

[58]Watzlawick et. al., op. cit., pp. 86–90.
[59]Laing, op. cit., pp. 135–136.
[60]G. Bateson et al., "Toward a Theory of Schizophrenia," Behavioral Science, 1 (1956), 251–264.

in which these elements occur: (1) for certain important reasons a person cannot withdraw from the scene; for example, for his own moral reasons he must continue to try to talk things over with his parents, or for his own religious reasons he must continue to try to talk with his wife; (2) messages are sent by the other person on the communication and metacommunication levels *which are internally contradictory on the two levels;* that is, the subject is validated by a verbal message and invalidated by metacommunication—those cues as to how he is to interpret the verbal message; and (3) his attempts at overt metacommunication about the contradiction are denied; that is, he is not allowed to initiate discussion about the internal contradiction posed between the verbal message which validates him and the nonverbal communication which invalidates him.

An attempt to justify the *denial* of opportunity to communicate about this contradiction, that is, denial of opportunity to engage in overt metacommunication about it, frequently is based on rather unreasonable grounds. Moral ground rules may be invoked: "It is not right (moral) for you to question your mother this way." Such morality is seldom expressed in overt verbal communication; rather the horrified stare or the hurt expression usually carry the message of infraction of moral boundaries. In other cases, an ethic is invoked; for example, in business circles it is sometimes claimed to be unethical to "deal in personalities." Thus a request for overt metacommunication about the contradiction may be construed as an attack on the other person's status or position of authority. Once again, refusal of overt metacommunication about the contradiction will likely be indicated by a cold stare or the nervous fidget rather than by forthright verbal communication.

If for his own reasons a person cannot "leave the field" and also is denied the opportunity to initiate overt metacommunication with the other person, he is confronted with an undecidable problem. If in addition he feels it is morally wrong to question the source of this contradiction, for example if he actually believes that it is immoral to question his mother about her confusing messages, he truly is in double bind. If he acts upon the apparent implication of the verbal message ("You are a worthwhile person or have a good idea," etc.) he will run the risk of antagonizing his mother. On the other hand if he accepts the apparent implication of his mother's vocal tone and general manner, he will infer that she thinks that his idea is worthless, and thus again will run the risk of antagonizing her by acting as if his mother did not "properly" care about her son. The point is, he is in trouble; he is "damned if he does and damned if he doesn't."

There is no way out of this dilemma; the doorways out—leaving the field, or initiating overt metacommunication—have been closed. In such a case the individual usually does one of three things: (1) He scans the interpersonal horizon, that is, his mother's behavior, for some message or clue that he must have missed or overlooked. (2) He does nothing; that is, he responds to nothing, ignores all or most communication from her or interprets all or most of her communication as of equal importance (or unimportance)—all confusing and all of slight value or meaning. (3) He may overreact, jumping inside his skin when his mother says, "How's my boy tonight?" Such is the way in which the double bind can produce an unhappy relationship between two more or less well-meaning people who, according to the notions of many of us, should mean a great deal to each other.

It is of the highest importance to note that the double bind is not life's ordinary difficult situation in which one must choose between two mutually exclusive but equally desirable alternatives, for example, choosing to be married or stay single, with both alternatives holding attraction, but once one is chosen, the other cannot then be enjoyed. The double bind is not the same dilemma; it is not a case of simply finding out you cannot have your cake and eat it too. Rather, in the case of the double bind, *both* choices are poor. *The double bind bankrupts choice itself;* neither alternative is tenable and the dilemma is complete—the situation is a true paradox.

Where double binding is of long-lasting duration it will produce an habitual expectation regarding the general nature of human relationships. This expectation leads to a self-perpetuating pattern of mistrust of communication. It can lead to alienation, not only toward others, but eventually toward oneself.[61]

[61]D. Jackson, "Psychoanalytic Education in the Communication Processes," *Science and Psychoanalysis,* 5 (1962), 129–145.

## Interpersonal Communication with the Alienated

There are few things more difficult than to try to overcome the effects of misuse of interpersonal communication principles outlined above; interaction with persons who have been alienated from their social environment is never easy. Of course, the primary requirement is that someone wants to make the effort. It is also helpful to provide the alienated person with insights into the process which has contributed to his alienation; sometimes this insight plus his own attempts to reach out annd establish new contacts with people around him tend to reduce the problem. *Most certainly, covert denial of communication must be avoided if interaction with alienated persons is to be achieved.*[62]

It has been our observation that people who alienate people and then are surprised at their alienation do not seem to understand very well the principles of interpersonal communication outlined above.

One can raise the following questions: When people alienate other people in the ways described are they really surprised by the results? Or are they perhaps subconsciously aware of what they are doing?

## SUMMARY

It should be emphasized that the purpose of the present analysis has not been to untangle the problems of all teen-agers, much less the snarls of the generation gap. Our purpose here has been simply to shed light on the way in which some persons are alienated from those who seem to be surprised when it happens. It is our belief that new insight into such a problem shows ways in which it can be reduced. Our suggestions regarding ways in which basic principles of interpersonal communication have been ignored or violated identifies possible changes in communication behavior which sometimes can provide more desirable results—warmer and more satisfying interpersonal relationships.

[62]K. Giffin and K. Bradley, "An Exploratory Study of Group Counselling for Speech Anxiety," *Journal of Clinical Psychology* 25 (1969), 98–101.

In this chapter we have described four very personal and basic barriers to effective interpersonal relations: lack of trust, defensiveness, prejudice between reference groups, and social alienation. We have explained ways in which such barriers are formed and suggested interpersonal communication techniques which can be used to avoid or reduce these barriers. Appropriate changes in one's communication behavior are more easily achieved if one has good insight into the need for such changes. In this rather lengthy chapter we have attempted to provide the basis for such insight.

## Suggested Applications and Learning Experiences

1. With one of your classmates take a "trust walk." Do it this way: close your eyes and have the other person lead or guide you out of the room and out-of-doors and around at least two objects such as a building and a tree; on the return trip have the other person close his eyes and you guide him. During this walk note very carefully two things: (1) ways in which the other person "takes care of you" and actually shows that he cares about you; (2) your own thoughts and feelings while the other person is dependent upon you. Discuss these observations with a small group of your classmates after they have returned from a similar "trust walk." Determine for yourself personally the extent to which you have perhaps previously been needlessly distrustful of other people or careless about trust placed in you by others.

2. Obtain permission to observe a routine problem-solving discussion such as that which frequently occurs in a dormitory or student living group, or student organization. Note very carefully any defensive behavior which occurs; also note the immediately preceding interaction which seemed to generate this defensiveness, and compare it with Gibb's findings reported in the preceding chapter. Share your observations with a small group of your classmates.

3. Select a person of your acquaintance who is at least twenty years older than you; arrange to have lunch together "to discuss the generation gap." During your lunch period do the following two things: (1) ask him to identify ways in which he believes you *think* differently from the ways he thinks (suggest possible differences in values and motivations), and (2) ask him to temporarily "exchange

places with you" as you and he *role-play* each other in a brief additional discussion of these human values and motivations. Identify new information thus obtained about the "older generation" and report it to your classmates. Note especially any changes of attitude (positive or negative) on your part as a result of this experience.

4. Determine in your own mind the degree to which you feel alienated from some particular person who is supposed to be (expected by society to be) important to you. This may be a wife, husband, mother, father, sister, brother, teacher, counselor, adviser, or department chairman. Arrange a meeting with such a person and note very carefully any evidences of *communication denial* on the part of this person; note also the nature of your responses to such denial. Carefully but deliberately attempt to discuss with this person your perception of his communication denial and what the two of you might be able to do about it. Share your findings with your classmates.

5. If for any reason (geographic distance or no feelings of alienation on your part) you cannot comply with suggestion 4 above, select a member of another race and follow the instructions given.

### Suggested Readings

Gibb, Jack, "Climate for Trust Formation," in Leland P. Bradford, Jack Gibb, and Kenneth D. Benne, eds., *T-Group Theory and Laboratory Method,* New York, Wiley, 1964, pp. 279–309.

*Gibb, Jack, "Defensive Communication," *Journal of Communication,* 11 (1961), 141–148.

*Giffin, Kim, and Bobby R. Patton, "Personal Trust in Human Interactions" *Basic Readings in Interpersonal Communication,* New York, Harper & Row, 1971.

Hajda, Jan, "Alienation and Integration of Student Intellectuals," *American Sociological Review,* 26 (1961), 758–777.

*Roethlisberger, F. J., "Barriers to Communication Between Men," paper presented October 11, 1951, at Northwestern Univ.'s Centennial Conference on Communications, and published in *ETC: A Review of General Semantics,* 10 (1952), 41–46.

Thibaut, J. W., and J. Cowles, "The Role of Communication in the Reduction of Interpersonal Hostility," *Journal of Abnormal and Social Psychology, 47* (1952), 770–777.

Watzlawick, Paul, Janet H. Beavin, and Don D. Jackson, *Pragmatics of Human Communication,* New York, Norton, 1967, pp. 13–71.

*Items thus identified are reprinted in Kim Giffin and Bobby R. Patton, *Basic Readings in Interpersonal Communication,* New York, Harper & Row, 1971.

# guidelines for effective interpersonal communication | 8

Advice is rarely popular, especially when it is not requested. Up to this point we have attempted to be explanatory and descriptive, relying upon available research conclusions on interpersonal communication. In this chapter, however, we shall be prescriptive—advice and suggestions will be offered based upon theories and concepts presented in previous chapters.

Obviously, you must use sound judgment in applying these suggestions. Interpersonal communication should never be mechanistic or routine. A suggestion that might be generally useful may not apply specifically to your communication with your father, mother, teacher, or particular friend. The value of the data here presented is to increase your awareness of choice in interpersonal encounters. The educated person should be cognizant of the communication choices available to him and the potential consequences.

The suggestions in this chapter are organized into units corresponding to the previous seven chapters, and provide the following background data.

1. The first section consists of general suggestions for the application of basic principles of interpersonal communication.
2. The second suggests ways of meeting our interpersonal needs through communication.
3. The third contains advice on achieving accurate perception of others.
4. The fourth provides help in evaluating our general orientation toward others.
5. The fifth identifies ways of searching for another person's meaning as he tries to talk with us.
6. Section six focuses on ways of adjusting to our interpersonal environment.
7. Suggestions for overcoming interpersonal barriers are given in the seventh unit.

We shall then conclude with suggestions for helping the other person as you try to improve your communication with him.

## 1. NOTE THE INFLUENCE OF BASIC FACTORS OF INTERPERSONAL COMMUNICATION

When we are with someone in a face-to-face situation, there are five basic interpersonal behaviors that must be recognized and evaluated in terms of their impact on our own behavior as well as that of the other person.

First, we must remember that we cannot *not* communicate. A refusal to talk with someone is a communication message. The unspoken give-and-take of human relations is often the most important part. The office worker's jealous defense of his desk is a communication in *time,* telling others exactly what he thinks of his privacy and position, and what he would like others to think of them. Likewise, the way in which we keep others waiting for an appointment, or are kept waiting by them, signifies our feelings of superiority, equality, or inferiority. A refusal to talk with someone amounts to a significant message.

Second, we should note the response of the other person to both the message we are sending and the information we give about the message. It is a mistake to assume that what we *tell* other people is what they will automatically believe—if they can see

that our expressions and gestures and general attitude do not agree with our spoken words. To the other person, reality lies in the total appearance, not in a verbal formula. The parent who preaches truth and tolerance but is sneaky in his behavior and bigoted by certain beliefs will likely find that his child is imitating his basic attitudes rather than his verbal declarations. When we say something to another person, we should learn to recognize clues and suggestions that indicate how that person is taking the message. Likewise, we should be able to reverse the process and attempt to be alert to the message about messages that we send nonverbally to others.

Third, when we are with someone in a situation where clear understanding is essential, we should frequently review what is going on. We must watch for ways in which the other person identifies parts of the interaction which has occurred. For example, they may say that they have been telling us about something. They may be punctuating the series of interactions by identifying themselves as the leader in the situation and us as the follower. We may feel that *we* have been telling *them* a number of things and that *they* are responding. The difference in the ways in which the two of us "punctuate" the series of interactions that have occurred can be significant.

Fourth, we must learn to recognize the ways our nonverbal behavior indicates our relationship with another person. It is quite possible that by nonverbal behavioral clues and cues another person tells us that he intends to relate to us in a way quite different from that which he suggests in his verbal messages. We must pay special attention to situations where the verbal and nonverbal behaviors are in contradiction. The problem then is to reconcile the disparity in the messages conveyed if the relationship is to be mutually understood.

Fifth, it is desirable in most cases to strive for a complementary rather than a competitive relationship. While some relationships are inevitably competitive, most of us find it more pleasant to develop one where each other's needs and satisfactions are complemented.

## 2. ATTEMPT TO MEET YOUR OWN INTERPERSONAL NEEDS THROUGH COMMUNICATION

Many of our individual needs can only be satisfied through social interaction; these include our personal development, personal growth, clarification of our relationships with others, and ways of negotiating our disagreements.

In our personal development we must deliberately search for new ways of gaining social approval. As our social environments change we need to check on those elements in them which earn approval. As we should avoid straight, narrow, ritualized ways of behaving, we should also avoid trying to hide a part of ourselves, or acting as if we are something which we are not. An open, frank, and genuine approach to others in our communication is our best avenue to self-identity.

We must build confidence in our ability to achieve and maintain self-esteem. This is accomplished as we expose a bit of ourselves to someone and note and evaluate the feedback we receive. As we find that we can profit from such exposure and feedback, we then expose ourselves a little more. When we find a person whom we can trust to be open, frank, and accepting, we can gain honest and genuine feedback. As we communicate in this fashion with another, we may achieve the pleasure of shared personal growth. When we can discuss ourselves and our relationships openly and frankly and even find that we can be comfortable in shared silence, we have achieved a level of interpersonal growth which is fully worth the effort.

When we have associated with other individuals over a period of time, there is a temptation to take the relationships for granted. In a work group, it is often useful to ask the other people how they feel about the way the members work together. A conflict area or basis of confusion may be revealed. We should seek to establish a pattern whereby every now and then we seek to clarify our relationships with those with whom we come in constant contact.

We should negotiate disagreements by attempting to achieve a level of mutual satisfaction. Ethically, we should avoid deliberate efforts to manipulate or distort the perceptions of others. They may see things differently than we do, but we should allow this to occur and attempt to understand it. The bases for our varying perceptions should be communicated, and mutual revision accomplished, particularly if our needs and desires are obscuring reality. A compromise is sometimes necessary; usually it can be satisfactorily achieved through open, accurate, and honest exposure of the different viewpoints.

## 3. TRY TO ACHIEVE ACCURATE PERCEPTIONS OF OTHER PERSONS

We should attempt to avoid use of pigeonhole categories and oversimplification in our perceptions of other people. We must expect and note complexities and differences instead of simple similarities. We should expect our perceptions of another person to change from time to time, and avoid "once-and-for-all" conclusions. Two-valued orientations such as "clean-dirty," "old-young," and status perceptions like "high-low," should not fllter our views of others.

It is important to watch for subtle visual cues as we try to get to know others better. It will be necessary to look beyond such surface characteristics as use of cosmetics, long hair, and dress; as we avoid misleading stereotype-casting we should watch closely for visual expressions and slight changes in posture and eye contact that give us more significant messages. Such metacommunication can help us understand the emotions and true feelings of the other person. We may deliberately have to explore the ways in which he wishes to relate to us, or the "game" which he is attempting to play.

## 4. UNDERSTAND YOUR INTERPERSONAL ORIENTATION TOWARD OTHER PEOPLE

It is important that we try to understand the ways in which we ordinarily interact with others. Such an orientation may serve our own personal needs for interaction, but greater flexibility may serve them even better.

One of the major considerations is to determine if our willingness to interact with others is congruent with our desire to be included in their activities. Occasionally we find an unhappy person who, for one reason or another, is unwilling to include others in his life or activities, and at the same time feels that others seem to pass him by. The "Golden Rule" would seem to apply, for if we wish others to include us in their activities, we will have to show the same interest in including them in ours.

We must determine if we are willing to share control of a group in which we participate. We must see if our desire to control others is balanced by a willingness to be controlled at times by them. If we attempt to control others and feel that we can be happy only if we are in control of the situation, we may find conflict with those who are unwilling to let us control all of the time. It is probably beneficial to adopt a balanced approach, to be willing to be controlled as well as to be willing to take control when others seem to feel that it is appropriate.

Similarly, we should determine if our needs to receive attention and affection are approximately equal to our tendencies of showing affection to others. This area is critical in interpersonal orientations. In our culture, many of us, especially males, find it difficult to show affection toward others. At the same time, however, most men and boys find it pleasant and rewarding to receive attention and affection. The point is this: if we want affection from others, we will probably have to be willing to show it toward *them* at appropriate times. Such displays of affection may be so foreign to our nature as to be awkward or even embarrassing, but it may be necessary if our interpersonal relations are to be mutually pleasant and satisfying.

In sum, if we feel that if we are left out of groups or given too little attention or affection by others, we can do the following:

a. Make a special effort to include others in our circle of associates;
b. Show more readiness to accept the leadership and suggestions of others; and
c. Sincerely show to others the genuine affection which we feel for them.

We must try to bring our behavior toward others into congruence with the interpersonal behavior that we would like to have them extend to us.

## 5. SEARCH FOR THE OTHER PERSON'S MEANING WHEN HE TRIES TO TALK WITH YOU

If we are to gain maximum information from our interactions, we have to avoid making fast assumptions that we "know what he means." Whereas the metacommunication and nonverbal signals provide clues to the other person's intended meanings, we should ask for additional information when the cues are in conflict or if we are unsure what is intended. We must make every attempt to make certain that our conceptual maps are known to one another and that they fit the territory they purport to represent.

We should pay special attention to the intended meaning of another person when he uses words describing such strong feelings as love, dislike, hurt, sympathy, understanding, and fear. When a person says that he is afraid of something or when he says he is unhappy with someone, we must not automatically assume we know what he means. Our own experiences and feelings may make empathy difficult.

Sudden shifts in the levels of abstraction should be noted. Suppose we ask a friend, "Did you have a good time at the party last night?" and he responds, "I met a lot of new people." Since we asked for an evaluative response and received a statement of fact, what conclusions can we draw?

Since language can be used as an instrument for interpersonal manipulation, we should be alert to the ways in which we are influenced and persuaded. Consider the ways in which many adults talk to children: basic premises are implied but not stated openly; value systems are evoked but not discussed; general statements are made about observed data, behaviors, and events but are not allowed to be questioned. For example, a child may want to wear his hair long, and his mother states, "Boys don't look good with long hair; men don't wear long hair; only beatniks and hippies run around with hair hanging down on their shoulders; I don't want to discuss it further." Such a statement negates the possibility of discussion of such questions as: (1) Long hair looks bad to *whom?* (2) Has long hair never been worn by some admirable men? (3) Are beatniks and hippies all "bad"? An open invitation to discuss the relative importance of adherence to social customs would be a mature, ethical way to approach this example of interpersonal conflict or disagreement. Avoidance of such discussion on grounds that the child is "too young" for such interaction voids the opportunity to help him grow and develop—it also denies the actual facts of the situation which initiated the conflict.

Such uses of language are manipulative and produce responses which may be unthinkingly submissive, resentful, alienated, or hostile. Interpersonal relationships are damaged rather than improved. Although it may be true that language is a social tool, care must be exercised that you or someone else are not thus "tooled."

Listening to others ordinarily requires deliberate effort. It should include a sincere attempt to understand the viewpoint of the other person: his value system, the source of his basic premises that frequently are implied but not openly stated; his generalized notion of observable facts, including his limited ability to observe objectively —sometimes called "personal prejudice"; and his limited linguistic ability to express his ideas in ways easily understood by others.

True listening is hard work. We may decide that in many cases it may not be worth all that much effort; but to make such a decision with full knowledge of the potential loss of understanding is one thing, and to allow such loss through ignorance is quite another. When we really desire a lasting relationship with someone, listening to him is a necessary investment.

The point of this discussion is this: a rewarding relationship with another person seldom occurs by chance; we can't expect such a relationship to "just happen." If we really want to enjoy being with another person, we have to work at "being with" him. A starting point is to try to listen, to hear with "ears like theirs" instead of ours.

## 6. TO ACHIEVE A DESIRED RELATIONSHIP WITH OTHERS, YOU MUST NOTE THE REQUIREMENTS OF VARIOUS SOCIAL SITUATIONS

Teachers of public speaking have for many years requested students to note the requirements of the "occasion" or the situation confronting a speaker. In like manner, in an interpersonal situation the other person expects us to interact in certain ways; these expectations will be related to the specific environment and the chain of events or interactions which have led to this specific encounter. We typically respond without reflecting upon the basis for our situational behavior.

We are here concerned with situations that call for discriminating choice, for fine distinctions. For example, you are going to accuse your roommate of misuse of your typewriter; at the time you meet him he is tired and frustrated by an ill-conceived assignment in chemistry. "Now is probably not the right time to bring it up, but—" is a poor way to bring it up if we want optimum response. There may never be a perfect time to open a discussion about personal disagreements, but the usual mistake is that they are not brought up early, that they are allowed to slide along until pent-up pressures explode them into the open. A presentation of such problems should take advantage of situational conditions that are at least somewhat favorable.

Certain situational guidelines are available for work in groups. We would hope to work with groups which provide optimum conditions for the accomplishment of a given task as well as maintaining positive group relations:

a. The group task should be clear and relevant to your interests;
b. There should be the possibility for you to achieve a desirable status in the group;
c. The group's norms should be known and acceptable to you;
d. The power structure of the group should offer you an opportunity to participate in controlling other members as well as being controlled and influenced;
e. Group cohesiveness should be present or potentially possible;
f. Leadership roles should be shared and there should be some possibility for you to achieve such a role; and
g. The personalities of most of the group members should be reasonably attractive to you—that is, few members should exhibit excessive anxieties or need to dominate others.

In joining and working with groups it may take some time to learn each of these group characteristics; and when we have done so, some elements may not be to our liking since, like people, few groups are perfect. However, if we are to work well with the group and achieve satisfaction, we will want most of the cited characteristics to be present or attainable.

## 7. MAKE A SPECIAL EFFORT TO OVERCOME SPECIAL BARRIERS TO INTERPERSONAL COMMUNICATION

None of us is likely to be confronted with all the barriers cited in Chapter 7, but presence of any one can pose serious difficulties. Some general guidelines are self-evident.

Without allowing ourselves to become dupes for "confidence men," we should strive to increase our trust of other people. Increased trust in ourselves is vital; we must be willing to expose our thoughts and ideas to others and listen to their responses to these ideas. Our trust of others will increase as we learn to profit from their responses. An open and frank expression of what we think and how we feel about it will be an excellent start to increasing interpersonal trust.

Our confidante must be selected with care. By easy stages we can achieve greater candor and disclosure of our feelings—our fears, anxieties, hopes, and pleasures. We should not worry about "saying things just right"; the other person's responses should guide us in determining how well we have expressed ourselves. As trust increases, we will learn that the correction of misinterpretation is not only possible but relatively easy; it does require, however, that we listen carefully to the other person's responses to and reflections upon our thoughts.

The most valuable thing for us to learn as our trust of others is increased is that *we do not lose self-esteem by self-disclosure and relevant feedback;* rather the opposite is true: *the surest way to increase self-esteem is to listen and to evaluate feedback about yourself from someone you trust, making changes in your behavior when desirable and possible.* In this way increased interpersonal trust serves our own personal needs and purposes.

We should try to reduce our own defensiveness as we attempt to interact with others. From time to time in verbal interaction almost everyone feels the need to defend himself; however, we should make a special effort to avoid use of defensive strategies, particularly distortion of comments made by others and personal attacks on others when we feel threatened. In most cases we really need not be defensive—the perceived threat is more imaginary than real; and when our self-image really is threatened, the strategies of distortion and counter-attacks actually *increase* the need for defending ourselves rather than reducing it.

In striving to reduce our own defensiveness, we will need to work with one or more persons in a mutual effort to provide a climate of interpersonal trust for each other. To accomplish this, we should try to talk in ways which are:

a. Descriptive rather than evaluative (withhold criticism temporarily),
b. Problem-oriented rather than directed toward control of each other,
c. Openly spontaneous rather than strategic or manipulative of each other's thoughts or ideas,
d. Empathic rather than strictly neutral or rigidly "objective,"
e. Indicative of personal equality rather than minor differences in status, and
f. Expressive of temporarily held viewpoints rather than of absolute certainties.

We should seek to reduce barriers between ourselves and members of other reference groups. The primary effort required is to try to see any such person *as a person* rather than in terms of a *label* or one of a class or stereotype. Rather than responding to him as "people like that," we need to take a good look at him; we must listen with great care and try to take an open-minded, objective, openly inquisitive look—to see first and judge later. We must strive to understand the basis or source of any feelings of alienation.

Carefully observe the communication behavior of those persons toward whom *you* feel alienation; do this when you feel somewhat guilty or unhappy about such a feeling. For example, if you feel alienated from your father and think that a person *should not* feel so alienated, observe your father's communication behavior as you try to talk with him. Determine if you are receiving "double messages," that is, statements that say he likes or trusts you presented in a tone or manner of attitude indicating that he does not trust you very much.

Though other nations, cultures, and generations may have value systems different from yours, these are not necessarily "wrong." To understand their usefulness at *any point in time or place* is a start in bridging the interpersonal gap. To comprehend (not necessarily adopt) another person's value system is a basis for understanding his behavior—his strange (even frightening) appearance, his food, drink, manners, and customs.

It is entirely possible that you may have some feelings of alienation regarding your parents, your teachers, or those persons in charge of your dormitory or living group. How do *you* respond to feelings of alienation? It is quite reasonable to withdraw (cut yourself off) from such interaction *unless* you wish to try to establish a better, more satisfying relationship with such persons. In such a case you still need to present a low-keyed, honest view of the situation as you see it. Indicate with as little emotion as possible your difficulty in responding to a "double message." Demonstrate your own good intentions toward the other person by making a determined effort to understand the thinking which produces such contradictory communication. Accept *as fact* the other person's ambivalence—his feelings of liking you *plus* dislike; his hopes *plus* his fear of being disappointed; his need for your acceptance of him as he is (ambivalent) *plus* his anxiety that your acceptance may be withheld. Such "double-messages" must be accepted as valuable modes of communication if we are to understand *both* of the apparently contradictory messages.

You may find that your attempts to discuss the problem are resisted; you may be denied the opportunity to talk it over. You may do your best and meet only a shrug of the shoulder or a change of topic—a response denying any willingness to talk with you about such things. You have thus met communication denial and you may as well recognize it for what it is. You have now been given a new message: that person is not ready to try to establish a better relationship with you. You must accept this *as fact,* and decide whether or not you want to make further efforts in that direction. It is sad to acknowledge that not every father (or mother or teacher) is really capable of working with you toward establishing a close, friendly relationship. His personal needs, social anxieties, or fear of damage to his self-esteem may be too great for him to risk the attempt. He may need your help but be unable to accept it.

Helping others to improve their interpersonal relations is not easy; it requires specific interpersonal attitudes and behavior. For this reason, the final section of this book is devoted to the problem of helping the other person as you try to improve your relationship with him.

## 8. TRY TO HELP THE OTHER PERSON BY SHOWING ACCURATE EMPATHY, NONPOSSESSIVE WARMTH, AND GENUINENESS

Another person will need your help in his effort to establish better interpersonal relationships when he fears exposure of his ideas and feelings. What he actually fears is possible damage to his self-image as a result of this exposure. He will need to build his self-esteem by expressing his ideas and feelings and then attempting to change his behavior in view of what he judges to be valid feedback from others. He will need your help in overcoming this fear.

He may not feel that he needs your help. He may not properly understand his need or problem; he may resent the idea of needing assistance or consideration from anyone. If he fails to recognize this need, you may make the mistake of trying to point it out to him. Such effort is likely to be ineffective because it will tend to *increase* his anxiety—the source of his difficulty in the first place. Many times this problem is simply aggravated by persons who try to be "helpful," but are not very knowledgeable.

What is a helping relationship? What can be done for such a person? You can seek to provide what Rogers called a sense of psychological safety,[1] also described by Gibb as a climate of trust formation.[2] You can give him the opportunity to test his ideas and attitudes in a nonthreatening social environment.

What should you actually do to provide such a supportive climate? Studies of counselors and therapists, summarized by Truax and Carkhuff,[3] indicate differences in the relationship between coun-

[1] C. R. Rogers, *Client-Centered Therapy,* Boston, Houghton Mifflin, 1951.
[2] J. R. Gibb, "Climate for Trust Formation," in P. Bradford, J. R. Gibb, and K. D. Benne, eds., *T-Group Theory and Laboratory Method: Innovation in Re-Education,* New York, Wiley, 1964, pp. 279–309.
[3] C. B. Truax and R. R. Carkhuff, *Toward Effective Counseling and Psychotherapy,* Chicago, Aldine, 1967.

selors and clients. Specifically, counselors vary as to characteristics of accurate empathy, nonpossessive warmth, and genuineness. These studies have demonstrated that counselors who show higher degrees of these particular characteristics have greater success with clients in psychiatric hospitals, out-patient clinics, veterans clinics, college counseling centers, and juvenile delinquency institutions. The studies include both individual and group counseling approaches. These findings appear to have direct application in all interpersonal communication situations involving a need for understanding.

Accurate empathy is the ability to sense the other person's view of the world as if that view were your own. However, to *show* accurate empathy requires verbal ability to *communicate* this understanding to the other person.[4] You will need to be sensitive to his current feelings and emotions, even his fear of letting you develop a closer relationship with him. You need not *share* his feelings; that is, you do not need to feel the same fear or anxiety he does. But you must have an awareness and appreciation of these emotions. You must be able to sense feelings which are only partially revealed by the other person—emotions of which he is only partly aware. You must be able to clarify and expand his awareness of these feelings. Such empathy is communicated by the language you use and also by your vocal qualities and characteristics. Your posture, gestures, and entire attitude should reflect the other person's point of view and depth of feeling. Your behavior must show awareness of shifts in his emotional attitudes, his subtle fears and anxieties. At all times the message of accurate empathy is, "I am with you; I understand."

Nonpossessive warmth is a demonstration of unconditional positive regard; it involves caring about the other person without imposing conditions.[5] The attitude you communicate should be warm acceptance without evaluation; there should be no expression of dislike, disapproval, or conditional warmth in a selective or evaluative way. You will need to show willingness to share the other person's joys and aspirations as well as his anxiety and despair. It may be difficult for you to understand how you can really show warmth and affection for a person who has ways or habits you dislike—this is indeed a serious problem and becomes the heart of the matter in

[4]*Ibid.*, p. 46.
[5]*Ibid.*, p. 58.

trying to be helpful to others. What is actually required is caring about that person's *potential,* a warm feeling about him as a person —a human being. Hopefully, you and he *together* can face his problem, one which both of you dislike. But it is imperative that he feel you will be for him, even if he fails in his attempt to change his behavior or meet his problem. He will need to feel that you care very much about him regardless of his behavior. The attitude described here may not be very clear to you; indeed, in working with problems in human relations it is the most complicated concept we have faced. However, it is also the most important. Let us note it once again; nonpossessive warmth involves unconditional caring about a person *as a person with valued potential* irrespective of some behaviors which you do not like. You must show that you care for him even though you may not care for some of his ways. This caring is much like the loyalty and affection shown by supporters of a football team even when that team is having problems and losing games; these fans want the team to win, but they still love it when losing— they love it for trying and for its potential. If you wish to help another person you must show him acceptance as a human being who has both human frailties and human potential.

*Genuineness* consists of being open and frank at all times; it involves being yourself. You must not only be willing to express your feelings, but never to deny them.[6] There must be no facade, no defensive communication, no show of emotion which is followed by denial of that emotion. Your responses to the other person must be sincere, never phony. It does not mean that you need to show all of your feelings or emotions; but once one is shown, it must not be denied—your behavior must be congruent. You need not disclose your total self, but whatever is shown must be a real aspect of yourself, not behavior growing out of defensiveness or an attempt to *manipulate* the other person. Glib attempts to persuade him or efforts to convince him are dangerous pitfalls. A "professional" facade, "Now, let us take our medicine," can be disastrous. In view of the discussion of nonpossessive warmth in the preceding paragraph, it should be noted that your show of warmth must be genuine. This combination of requirements makes it extremely difficult to help another person if you really do not care about him. What you think

[6]*Ibid.,* pp. 68–69.

are clever strategies will likely be viewed with suspicion. You must learn to be truly yourself if you wish to be helpful to others.

## SUMMARY

It cannot be overemphasized that attempts to help others who do not wish your help are generally doomed to failure. Your efforts will only elicit suspicion and heightened distrust. Your best intentions will be misinterpreted, and you will all too easily become frustrated and disgusted. The other person must *want* your help for you to succeed in being helpful.

It is far from easy to be helpful to others. Even when they want your assistance, you will need great patience. You will need to be strong in your purpose to withstand failure and discouragement. You must be able to give accurate empathy—to understand the other person's viewpoint, to "stand in his shoes." You must care a lot about him if you are to show nonpossessive warmth. And you must be genuine—true to yourself, respectful of yourself, and self-confident —in order to be open and frank. None of these requirements is easy.

On the other hand, although it is not easy to be helpful to others, it is rewarding. It provides the best kind of opportunity for our own growth and development as a person. It provides a sense of personal joy and satisfaction. It illustrates the cardinal principle in interpersonal relations, a corollary of the "Golden Rule": whatsoever you do unto others, you also do unto yourself.

## Suggested Applications and Learning Experiences

1. The conceptual material presented in this chapter is comprised for the most part of prescribed behaviors which are handled descriptively in the first seven chapters. Thus, any of the Suggested Applications and Learning Experiences previously offered will apply to one or another section of Chapter 8. We strongly urge the reader to review the suggestions given following each of the first seven chapters and follow out any suggestions which have not been utilized. Note their relationship to those behaviors more formally prescribed in this last chapter.

2. The essentially new material in Chapter 8 concerns ways in which one person may attempt to help another in improving the latter's ways of relating to other people. The suggestion given here and the one in item 3 which follows are designed to make more clear and personal your learning about helping others and utilizing their help when offered. To give you more personal insight about helping others we offer the following suggestion. Determine which one of your friends or classmates would like to work with you on improving his ways of relating to others—this person will likely be one who has participated with you on one of the applications or learning experiences previously suggested in this book. Have that person meet with you and a third person for lunch. During this time have your friend do his best to employ effective interpersonal communication with this third person, while you act primarily as an observer. Later meet with your friend and give him open, frank, honest feedback on his behavior while talking at lunch. Then ask your friend to evaluate *your* communication behavior during the present discussion with respect to his perceptions of your *empathy, nonpossessive warmth,* and *genuineness.* Discuss these aspects of yourself with him at some length, being careful to listen more than you talk. At a later time when you are alone reflect on this feedback, recalling as best you can your own interpersonal communication behavior. Decide what specific behaviors you would like to change. Then arrange another similar sequence of experiences with two other persons. See if you can achieve feedback which is more desirable from your own point of view.

3. Identify that person who has shown you the greatest amounts of *empathy, warmth,* and *genuineness* while working with friends or classmates on applications and learning experiences suggested in this book. Ask him to meet with you and a *third* person for lunch. During this lunch period do your best to use effective interpersonal communication with the third person while your special friend acts mainly as an observer of your communication behavior. At a later meeting with your friend ask him for open and honest feedback regarding your behavior. Now, *note very carefully your personal feelings* as you listen to this friend criticize your effectiveness. Note any feelings of yours which are *negative or evasive. Note:* do you look your friend in the eye as you receive this feedback? Note

carefully any *defensive communication* on your part, identified either by you or by him. Thank your friend sincerely for his efforts to be of help to you. At a later time—the next day or in days to follow— determine for yourself your own capability for accepting and utilizing such help from other people.

## Suggested Readings

*Bales, Robert F., "In Conference," *Harvard Business Review, 32* (1954), 44–50.

Bennis, Warren G., et al., "Personal Change through Interpersonal Relationships," *Interpersonal Dynamics,* 2d ed., Homewood, Ill., Dorsey, 1968, pp. 333–369.

*Buchanan, Paul C., "How Can 'We' Gain 'Their' Commitment?" *Personnel, 40* (1965), 211–218.

Carson, Robert C., "Contractual Arrangement in Interpersonal Relations," *Interaction Concepts of Personality,* Chicago, Aldine, 1969, pp. 172–217.

*Rogers, Carl R., "The Characteristics of a Helping Relationship," *On Becoming A Person,* Boston, Houghton Mifflin, 1961, pp. 39–58.

Truax, Charles B., and Robert R. Carkhuff, *Toward Effective Counseling and Psychotherapy,* Chicago, Aldine, 1967, pp. 385–435.

Watson, Goodwin, "Resistance to Change," in Warren G. Bennis, Kenneth D. Benne, and Robert Chin, eds., *The Planning of Change,* 2d ed., New York, Holt, Rinehart and Winston, 1969, pp. 488–498.

*Items thus identified are reprinted in Kim Giffin and Bobby R. Patton, *Basic Readings in Interpersonal Communication,* New York, Harper & Row, 1971.

# index

Perception *(Continued)*
  cues, 70
  factor of common experience, 72
  capacities of, 71
  change in, 57
  children, 73, 106
  comunication, 99
  definition of, 57
  distortion of, 51–52, 66, 204
  formation of, 56
  interpersonal, 15, 20, 23, 52
  listener, 164
  mental set, 60
  of others, 170, 202
  parental, 73
  personal, 56–57, 69, 72
  process of, 57
  of relationship, 190
  of self, 73–74
    Negroes, 74
  sensory, 165
  social, 56, 72, 74
  trust, role of perception in, 163
    *See also* Trust, interpersonal
Personality, 95, 119
  behavioral patterns of, 80
  changes in, 176
  definition of, 78
  development of, 160
  dimensions of, 78, 155
  formation of impressions, 58
  group members, 154, 209
  problems of, 73
  traits, 67
Piaget, Jean, 106
Poitier, Sidney, 63
Power-structure, 149
  and communication flow, 150
Prejudice, 127
  personal, 208
    *See also* Stereotyping
*Presentation of Self in Everyday Life, The,* (Goffman), 33
Pretense, 33–36

Productivity in groups, 143
Propaganda, 129–130
Protestant Ethic, 181

Reference group, 20, 23
  definition of, 178
  gaps in, 180
Reflexes, interpersonal, 95
  manner, 95
Relationship, helping, *see* Helping relationship
  marital, 190
  parent-child, 189, 203
Reliability, 163, 169
Response, 31, 95
  emotional, 48
  interpretation of, 31
  reciprocal interpersonal responses, 95
  reflex, 93
  -training, 98
*Rhetoric* (Aristotle), 163
Ritual, 204
Rogers, Carl, 27, 135, 160, 162, 168, 213
Roles, 14, 34, 45, 98
  authority, 46
  functions of, 151
  leadership, 209
  participant, 44
  patterns, 95
  perceptions of, 45
  -playing, 35
    example of, 33
    metacommunication in, 36
  in small groups, factors determining, 151
  status, 152
Russia, 129, 140, 179, 183
  control techniques of, 129
    *See also* Soviets

Sansom, William, 33
Schutz, William, 98, 155
Self, hiding parts of, 31–33

designed by michel craig
set in optima
composed by v & m typographical, inc.
printed by the murray printing company
bound by book press
harper & row, publishers                    71  72  73  7  6  5  4  3  2